Claire Steep

Nelson

WORLD

ATLAS

FOURTH EDITION

REVIEWERS

James R. Crewe, Program Specialist
Avalon East School Board
St. John's, Newfoundland

Lew French, Program Supervisor
London Board of Education
London, Ontario

Kathryn Galvin, Principal
Calgary Board of Education
Calgary, Alberta

Robena Maclaren, Teacher
Bradshaw Elementary
Langley School District # 35
Langley, British Columbia

Nelson
Thomson Learning™

Australia • Canada • Denmark • Japan • Mexico • New Zealand • Philippines
Puerto Rico • Singapore • South Africa • Spain • United Kingdom • United States

I(T)P® **International Thomson Publishing**
The ITP logo is a trademark under licence
www.thomson.com

Published in 1998 by

I(T)P® **Nelson**

A division of Thomson Canada Limited
1120 Birchmount Road
Scarborough, Ontario M1K 5G4
www.nelson.com

Cartography by Philip's
© 1998 George Philip Limited
All rights reserved

Printed and Bound in Canada
 4 5 6 TCP 03 02

Canadian Cataloguing in Publication Data

George Philip Limited
Nelson world atlas

4th ed.
Includes index.
Earlier ed., 1991, by Geoffrey J. Matthews.
ISBN 0-17-607538-0

1. Atlases, Canadian. I Matthews, Geoffrey J.,
1932. Nelson world atlas. II. Title.

G1021.G469 1998   912   C98-900338-8

The publisher gratefully acknowledges the educators who gave us their comments and suggestions in our geography survey.

Project Team: Angela Cluer, Mark Cobham, Susan Cox, Deborah Crowle, Vicki Gould, Renate McCloy, Allan Moon, Theresa Thomas

Credits:
Page 48 California, USA (Science Photo Library - Earth Satellite Corporation), The Alps (Science Photo Library - NASA), Bangkok, Thailand (Science Photo Library - CNES/SPOT image), Nile Delta, Egypt (Getty Images - Nigel Press); Page 49 Saudi Arabia Irrigation (Science Photo Library - CNES/SPOT image), Winnipeg Floods (RADARSAT data © Canadian Space Agency/Agence spatiale canadienne 1997. Received by the Canada Centre for Remote Sensing. Processed and distributed by RADARSAT International. Enhancement and interpretation by Vantage Point International in cooperation with CCRS Geomatics Canada, The Great Lakes (Science Photo Library), London, UK (Science Photo Library–NRSC LTD.)

Contents

What is a Map?

These small maps explain the meaning of some of the lines and colours on the atlas maps.

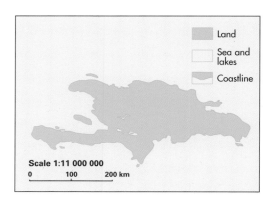

1. Land and sea
This is how an island is shown on a map. The land is coloured green and the sea is blue. The coastline is a blue line.

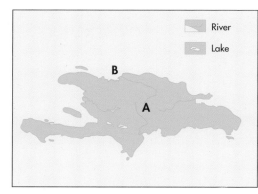

2. Rivers and lakes
There are some lakes on the island and rivers that flow to the sea. If you follow a river from its source (A) to the sea (B), you can tell that the river flows from higher to lower ground.

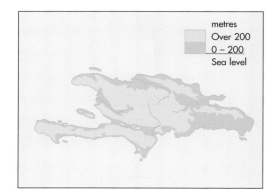

3. Height of the land – 1
This map shows the land over 200 metres high in a lighter colour. The height of the land is shown by layer colours and contour lines. The colour changes as the river flows to the sea.

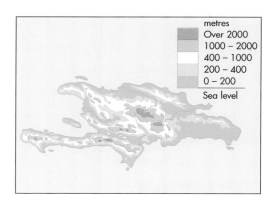

4. Height of the land – 2
This map shows more contour lines and layer colours. It shows that the highest land is in the centre of the island and that it is over 2000 metres high.

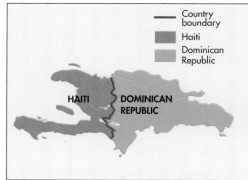

5. Countries
This is a way of showing different information about the island. It shows that the island is divided into two countries. They are separated by a country boundary.

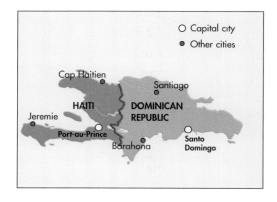

6. Cities and towns
There are cities and towns on the island. The two capital cities are shown with a special symbol. Other large or important cities are also shown.

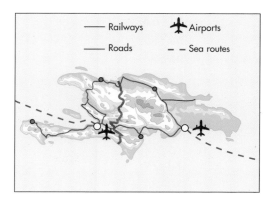

7. Transportation information
This map shows the most important roads, railways, airports and sea routes. Transportation routes connect the cities and towns.

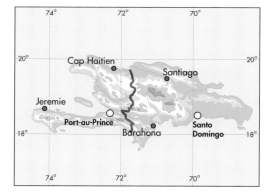

8. Where is the island?
This map gives the lines of latitude and longitude and shows where the island is in the world. Page 17 in the atlas shows the same island at a different scale.

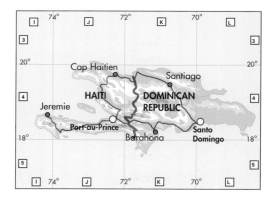

9. Location codes
This map includes the letter-figure codes used in the index. These letter-figure codes will help you locate a place on a map. The letter-figure code for Santiago is K4.

4

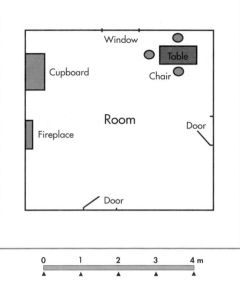

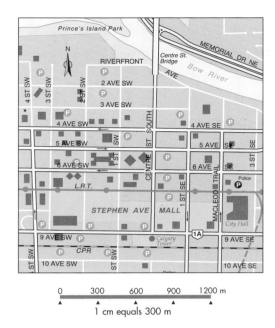

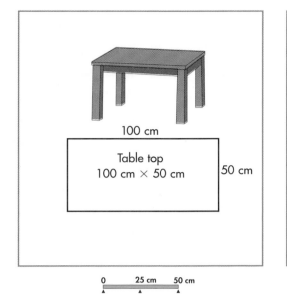

This is a drawing of the top of a table, looking down on it. It is 100 cm wide and 50 cm from front to back. The drawing measures 4 × 2 cm. It is drawn to scale: 1 cm on the drawing equals 25 cm on the table.

This is a plan of a room looking down from above. 1 cm on the map equals 1 metre in the room. The same table is shown, but now at a smaller scale. Use the scale bar to find the measurements of other parts of the room.

This is a map of an area in the city of Calgary. Large buildings can be seen but other buildings are too small to show. Below are atlas maps of different scales.

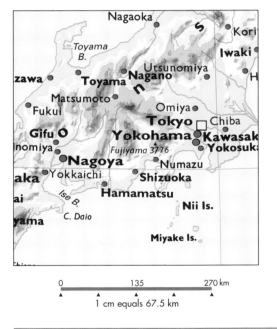

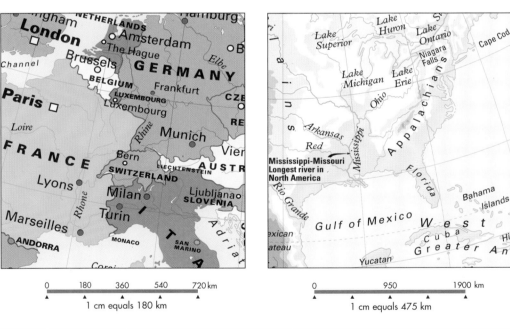

Types of scale
In this atlas the scale of the map is shown in three ways:

1. A written statement – this tells you how many kilometres on the Earth are represented by one centimetre on the map.

1 cm equals 20 km

2. Ratio – this tells you that one on the map represents two million of the same unit on the ground.

1 : 2 000 000

3. Scale – this shows you the scale as a line or bar with a section of ruler beneath it.

Direction

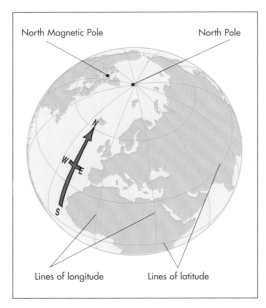

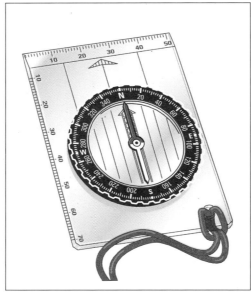

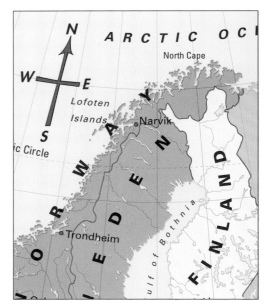

The Earth has a spot near the North Pole that is called the Magnetic Pole. If a piece of metal that was magnetized at one end was left to float, then the magnetized tip would point to the North Magnetic Pole.

The needle of a compass is magnetized and it always points north. If you know where you are and want to go to another place, you can measure your direction from a map and use a compass. Note the direction of this compass needle.

The compass or North Point shown on the map above indicates the direction of north. It points in the same direction as the lines of longitude. On the maps in this atlas, north is always at the top of the page.

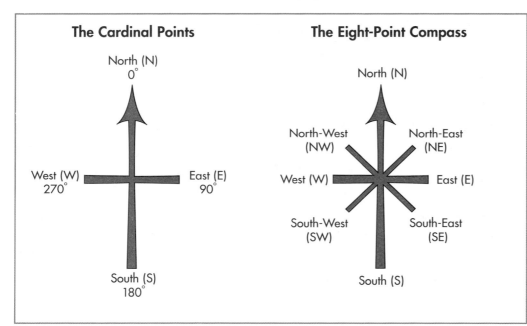

Direction is measured in degrees. The diagram above shows the degree numbers for each cardinal point. The direction is measured clockwise from north. The diagram on the right shows all the points of the compass and the divisions between the cardinal points. For example, between north and east there is north-east, between south and west is south-west. You can work out the cardinal points at your home by looking for the sun rising in the east and setting in the west.

This is part of the map on page 35. North is at the top. Look at the points of the compass on the diagram to the left and the positions of places on the map. Barcelona is north-east of Valencia and Marseilles is north-east of Barcelona. Think about the direction you would travel to go from Marseilles to Lyons.

Latitude and Longitude

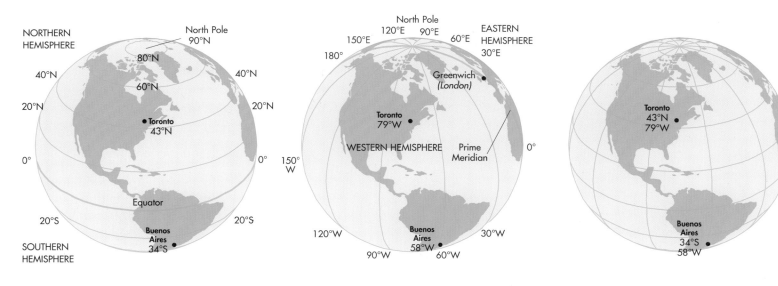

Latitude

This map shows how the Earth would look from thousands of kilometres above Toronto. The Equator is exactly halfway between the North and South Poles. It divides the Earth into two hemispheres. The Equator is shown as a line on maps. It is numbered 0°. There are other lines on maps north and south of the Equator. They are called lines of latitude.

Longitude

Maps have another set of lines running north to south linking the Poles. These lines are called lines of longitude. The line numbered 0° runs through Greenwich in London, England, and is called the Prime Meridian. The other lines of longitude are numbered up to 180° east and west of 0°. Longitude line 180° runs through the Pacific Ocean and is called the International Date Line.

Map references

The latitude and longitude lines on maps form a grid. In this atlas, the grid lines are in blue, and on most maps are shown for every ten degrees. The numbers of the lines can be used to give a reference to show the location of a place on a map. The index in this atlas uses another way of finding places. It lists the rows of latitude as numbers and the columns of longitude as letters.

Line of latitude with its number in degrees
Line of longitude with its number in degrees
Row number used in the index
Column letter used in the index

This table shows the largest city in each continent with its latitude and longitude. Look for them on the maps in this atlas.

	Latitude	Longitude	Map page	Map letter-figure
Cairo	30°N	31°E	**33**	F2
Moscow	56°N	38°E	**35**	Q4
New York	40°N	74°W	**23**	M2
Sao Paulo	24°S	48°W	**29**	F6
Shanghai	31°N	121°E	**45**	L3
Sydney	34°N	151°E	**31**	F11

The Earth as a Planet

Relative sizes of the planets

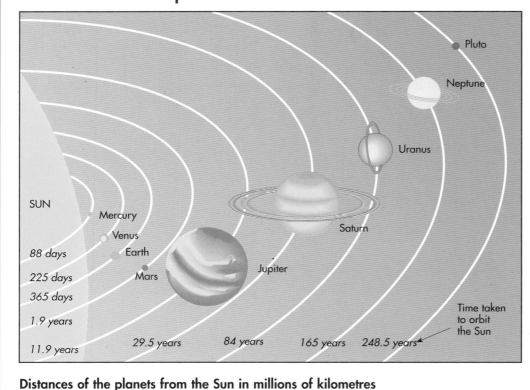

SUN

Mercury — 88 days
Venus — 225 days
Earth — 365 days
Mars — 1.9 years
Jupiter — 11.9 years
Saturn — 29.5 years
Uranus — 84 years
Neptune — 165 years
Pluto — 248.5 years

Time taken to orbit the Sun

The Solar System

The Earth is one of the nine planets that orbit the Sun. These two diagrams show the size of the planets, how far they are away from the Sun and how long they take to orbit the Sun. The diagram on the left shows that the planets closest to the Sun take the shortest time to orbit the Sun. The Earth takes 365 days (one year) to go round the Sun. The Earth is the fifth largest planet in the Solar System. It is much smaller than Jupiter and Saturn which are the largest planets.

Distances of the planets from the Sun in millions of kilometres

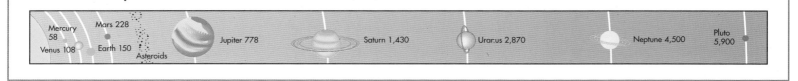

Mercury 58
Venus 108
Mars 228
Earth 150
Asteroids
Jupiter 778
Saturn 1,430
Uranus 2,870
Neptune 4,500
Pluto 5,900

Planet Earth

The Earth spins as if it is on a rod – its axis. The axis would come out of the Earth at two points. The northern point is called the North Pole and the southern point is called the South Pole. The distance between the Poles through the centre of the Earth is 12,700 km.

Equator — axis — North Pole

South Pole

This is the direction the Earth moves round its axis

It takes a day (24 hours) for the Earth to rotate once on its axis. It is light (day) when the Earth faces the Sun and dark (night) when it faces away. See the diagram below. The Equator is a line round the Earth which is halfway between the Poles. It is 40,000 km long.

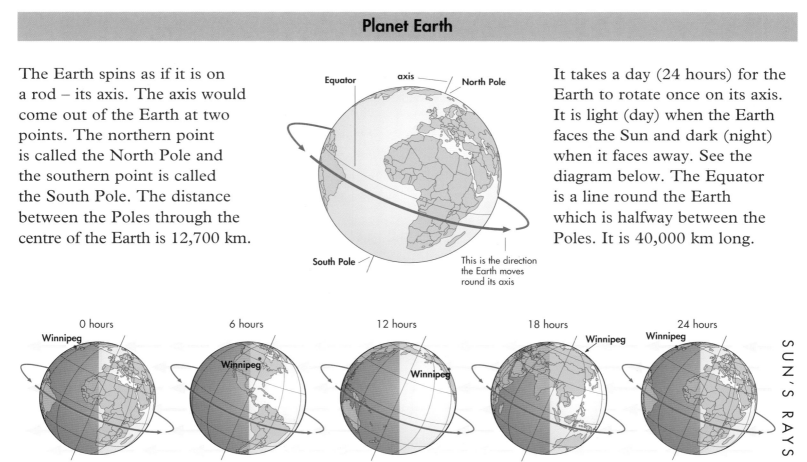

0 hours	6 hours	12 hours	18 hours	24 hours
Winnipeg	Winnipeg	Winnipeg	Winnipeg	Winnipeg
Midnight in Winnipeg	6 a.m. in Winnipeg	Noon in Winnipeg	6 p.m. in Winnipeg	Midnight in Winnipeg

SUN'S RAYS

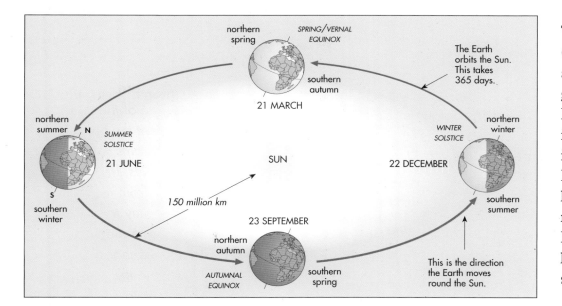

The Earth is always tilted at $66\frac{1}{2}°$ as it moves or rotates around the Sun. This movement gives us the seasons of the year. In June the northern hemisphere is tilted towards the Sun, so it is summer. Six months later, in December, the Earth has rotated halfway round the Sun and is now tilted away from the Sun. It is now winter in the northern hemisphere and summer in the southern hemisphere.

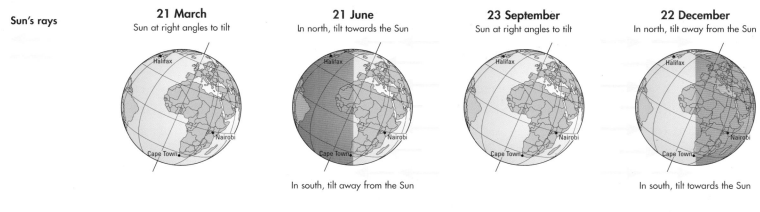

Season	Northern Spring Southern Autumn			Northern Summer Southern Winter			Northern Autumn Southern Spring			Northern Winter Southern Summer		
City	Halifax	Nairobi	Cape Town	Halifax	Nairobi	Cape Town	Halifax	Nairobi	Cape Town	Halifax	Nairobi	Cape Town
Latitude	44°N	1°S	34°S	44°N	1°S	34°S	44°N	1°S	34°S	44°N	1°S	34°S
Day length	12 hrs	12 hrs	12 hrs	15 hrs	12 hrs	10 hrs	12 hrs	12 hrs	12 hrs	9 hrs	12 hrs	14 hrs
Night length	12 hrs	12 hrs	12 hrs	9 hrs	12 hrs	14 hrs	12 hrs	12 hrs	12 hrs	15 hrs	12 hrs	10 hrs
Temperature	−1°C	21°C	21°C	14°C	18°C	13°C	15°C	19°C	14°C	−1°C	19°C	20°C

For example, at Halifax in spring and autumn there are 12 hours of day and 12 hours of night. In winter this becomes 9 hours and in the summer 15 hours.

The Moon

The Moon is about a quarter the size of the Earth. It orbits the Earth in just over 27 days (almost a month). The Moon is round but we on Earth see only the parts lit by the Sun. This makes it look as if the Moon is a different shape at different times of the month. These shapes are known as the phases of the Moon and they are shown in this diagram.

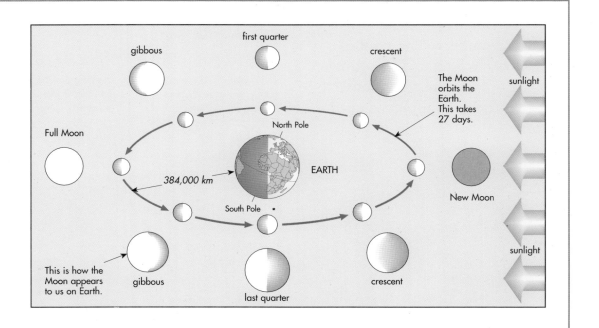

Map Information

Symbols

A map symbol shows the position of something – for example, trees for areas where lumbering is important.

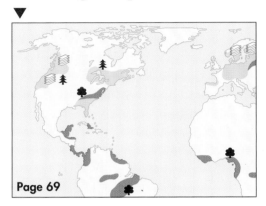

Page 69

On some maps a dot or a symbol stands for a large number – for example, the red dots stand for 2 million tonnes of wheat, the black dots 2 million tonnes of rice.

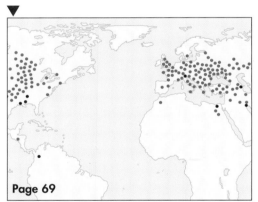

Page 69

The size of the symbol can be bigger or smaller, to show different numbers. The symbol here shows livestock. The squares are in proportion to the number of cattle, sheep, and pigs in each country.

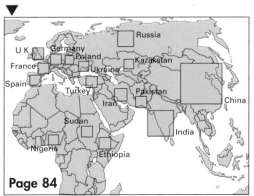

Page 84

Colours

1. Colours are used on some maps so that separate areas, such as countries, as in this map, can be seen clearly.

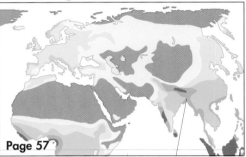

Page 35

3. Patterns on maps often spread across country borders. This map shows the different types of vegetation in the world.

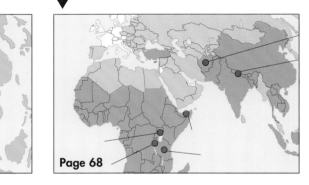

Page 66

2. On other maps, areas which are the same in some way have the same colour to show patterns. This map shows rainfall in different parts of the world.

Page 57

4. Colours that are lighter or darker are used on some maps to show less or more of something. This map shows areas where agriculture is important.

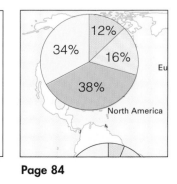

Page 68

Graphs and charts

Graphs and charts are used to give more information about subjects shown on the maps.

A graph shows how something changes over time.

This graph shows the rainfall and temperature for each month in a year which can be measured on the scale at the side of the graph.

This diagram is called a pie-chart. It shows how you can divide a total into its parts.

This is a bar-chart. It is another way of showing a total divided into parts.

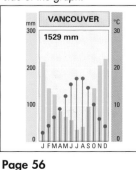

Page 56

Page 84

Page 85

10

MAP SYMBOLS

This is a slice through the map of the United States on pages 22 and 23. It is used here to explain the meaning of the lines, colours and symbols.

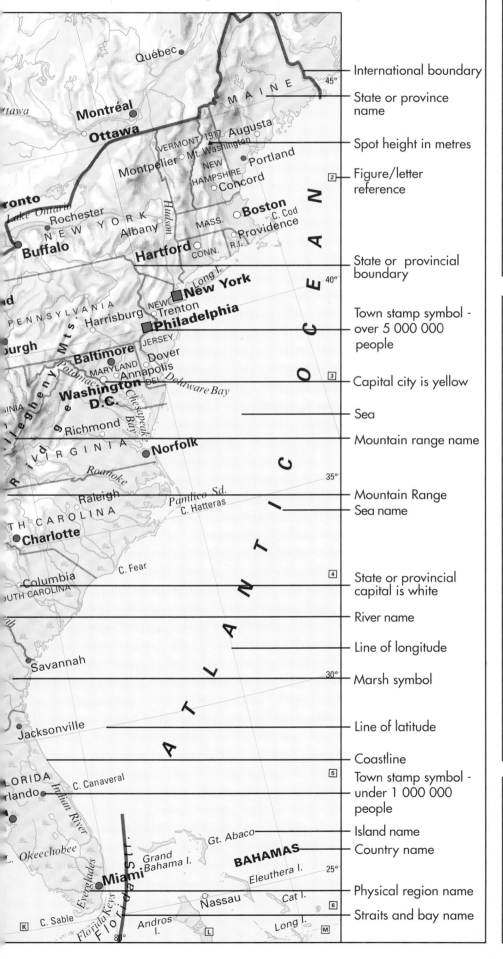

- International boundary
- State or province name
- Spot height in metres
- Figure/letter reference
- State or provincial boundary
- Town stamp symbol - over 5 000 000 people
- Capital city is yellow
- Sea
- Mountain range name
- Mountain Range
- Sea name
- State or provincial capital is white
- River name
- Line of longitude
- Marsh symbol
- Line of latitude
- Coastline
- Town stamp symbol - under 1 000 000 people
- Island name
- Country name
- Physical region name
- Straits and bay name

HEIGHT OF THE LAND & KEY

These explanation boxes appear on each map to show the height of the land above sea level and to explain some of the features on the map.

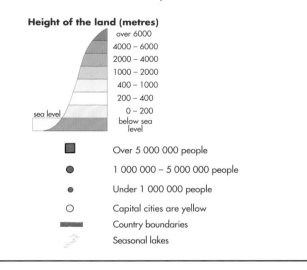

Height of the land (metres)

- over 6000
- 4000 – 6000
- 2000 – 4000
- 1000 – 2000
- 400 – 1000
- 200 – 400
- 0 – 200
- below sea level

sea level

- ◼ Over 5 000 000 people
- ● 1 000 000 – 5 000 000 people
- • Under 1 000 000 people
- ○ Capital cities are yellow
- ▬ Country boundaries
- Seasonal lakes

LOCATOR MAP

Locator maps are provided on each of the following pages:

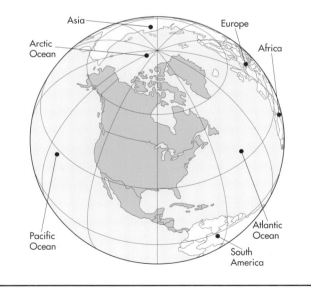

SCALE BAR

Scale 1:6 400 000   1cm on the map = 64km on the ground

| 0 | 64km | 128km | 192km | 256km | 320km | 384km | 448km |

cm ... cm

World – Physical

Height of the land (metres)

- over 4000
- 2000 – 4000
- 1000 – 2000
- 400 – 1000
- 200 – 400
- 0 – 200
- below sea level

sea level

Projection: Hammers Equal Area

Continent	Area, '000 km²	Coldest place, °C	Hottest place, °C	Wettest place (average annual rainfall, mm)	(average annual rainfall, mm)
Asia	44 500	Verkhoyansk, Russia -68°C ①	Tirat Zevi, Israel 54°C ⑧	Cherrapunji, India 11 430 ⑮	Aden, Yemen 46
Africa	30 302	Ifrane, Morocco -24°C ②	El Azizia, Libya 58°C ⑨	Debundscha, Cameroon 10 290 ⑯	Wadi Halfa, Sudan 2
North America	24 241	Snag, Yukon -63°C ③	Death Valley, California 57°C ⑩	Henderson Lake, Canada 6 500 ⑰	Bataques, Mexico 30
South America	17 793	Sarmiento, Argentina – 33°C ④	Rivadavia, Argentina 49°C ⑪	Quibdó, Colombia 8 990 ⑱	Arica, Chile 0.8
Antarctica	14 000	Vostok -89°C ⑤	Vanda Station 15°C ⑫		
Europe	9 957	Ust'Shchugor, Russia −55°C ⑥	Seville, Spain 50°C ⑬	Crkvice, Yugoslavia 4 650 ⑲	Astrakhan, Russia 160
Oceania	8 557	Charlotte Pass, Australia -22°C ⑦	Cloncurry, Australia 53°C ⑭	Tully, Australia 4 550 ⑳	Muika, Australia 100

CARTOGRAPHY BY PHILIP'S. COPYRIGHT REED INTERNATIONAL BOOKS LTD.

Continental boundaries

World - largest seas,	'000 km²		World - largest lakes,	'000 km²		World - longest rivers, km		World - largest islands,	'000 km²		World - highest peaks, m		World - deepest trenches, m	
cific Ocean 165 721	27		Caspian Sea 424	37		Nile 6 690	47	Greenland 2 176	57	Himalayas: Mt. Everest 8 848	67	Mariana Trench 11 022	77
antic Ocean 81 660	28		Lake Superior 82	38		Amazon 6 280	48	New Guinea 777	58	Karakoram Ra: K2 8 611	68	Tonga Trench 10 822	78
dian Ocean 73 442	29		Lake Victoria 69	39		Mississippi -Missouri 6 270	49	Borneo 725	59	Pamirs: Communism Pk. 7 495	69	Japan Trench 10 554	79
ctic Ocean 14 351	30		Lake Huron 60	40		Yangtze-Kiang 4 990	50	Madagascar 590	60	Tian Shan: Pik Pobedy 7 444	70	Kuril Trench 10 542	80
editerranean Sea 2 966	31		Lake Michigan 58	41		Congo 4 670	51	Baffin Island 476	61	Andes: Aconcagua 6 960	71	Mindanao Trench 10 497	81
uth China Sea 2 318	32		Aral Sea 36	42		Amur 4 410	52	Sumatra 474	62	Rocky Mts: Mt. McKinley 6 194	72	Kermadec Trench 10 047	82
ring Sea 2 274	33		Lake Tanganyika 33	43		Hwang-Ho 4 350	53	Honshu 228	63	East Africa: Mt. Kilimanjaro 5 895	73	Milwaukee Deep 9 200	83
ribbean Sea 1 942	34		Lake Baikal 31	44		Lena 4 260	54	Great Britain 217	64	Caucasus: Élbrus 5 633	74	Bougainville Trench 9 140	84
lf of Mexico 1 813	35		Great Bear Lake 31	45		Mekong 4 180	55	Victoria Island 212	65	Antarctica: Vinson Massif 5 139	75	South Sandwich Island Trench 8 428	85
a of Okhotsk 1 528	36		Lake Malawi 31	46		Niger 4 180	56	Ellesmere Island 197	66	Alps: Mt. Blanc 4 810	76	Aleutian Trench 7 822	86

13

Projection: Hammers Equal Area

Country	Population in thousands 1995 estimate	Area in thous' km²	Country	Population in thousands 1995 estimate	Area in thous' km²	Country	Population in thousands 1995 estimate	Area in thous' km²	Country	Population in thousands 1995 estimate	Area in thous' km²	Country	Population in thousands 1995 estimate	Area in thous' km²
China	1 226 944	9 597	Nigeria	88 515	924	Italy	57 181	301	Argentina	34 663	2 767	Uzbekistan	22 833	
India	942 989	3 288	Germany	82 000	357	Ukraine	52 027	604	Sudan	29 980	2 506	Nepal	21 953	
United States	263 563	9 373	Vietnam	74 580	332	Ethiopia	51 600	1 128	Canada	29 972	9 976	Venezuela	21 810	
Indonesia	198 644	1 905	Iran	68 885	1 648	Burma (Myanmar)	46 580	677	Tanzania	29 710	945	Uganda	21 466	
Brazil	161 416	8 512	Philippines	67 167	300	South Korea	45 088	99	Kenya	28 240	580	Taiwan	21 100	
Russia	148 385	17 075	Egypt	64 100	1 001	Congo (Dem. Rep. of the)	44 504	2 345	Algeria	27 936	2 382	Iraq	20 184	
Pakistan	143 595	796	Turkey	61 303	779	South Africa	44 000	1 220	Morocco	26 857	447	Malaysia	20 174	
Japan	125 156	378	Thailand	58 432	513	Spain	39 664	505	North Korea	23 931	121	Afghanistan	19 509	
Bangladesh	118 342	144	United Kingdom	58 306	243	Poland	38 587	313	Peru	23 588	1 285	Saudi Arabia	18 395	2
Mexico	93 342	1 958	France	58 286	552	Colombia	34 948	1 139	Romania	22 863	238	Sri Lanka	18 359	

14

Scale 1:80 000 000   1cm on the map = 800km at the Equator

Country	Population in thousands 1995 estimate	Area in thous' km²	Country	Population in thousands 1995 estimate	Area in thous' km²	Country	Population in thousands 1995 estimate	Area in thous' km²	Country	Population in thousands 1995 estimate	Area in thous' km²	Country	Population in thousands 1995 estimate	Area in thous' km²
stralia	18 107	7 687	Cameroon	13 232	475	Belarus	10 500	208	Tunisia	8 906	164	Haiti	7 180	28
ozambique	17 800	802	Zimbabwe	11 453	391	Czech Republic	10 500	79	Sweden	8 893	450	Guinea	6 702	246
ana	17 462	239	Ecuador	11 384	284	Hungary	10 500	93	Bulgaria	8 771	111	Burundi	6 412	28
zakstan	17 099	2 717	Cuba	11 050	111	Cambodia	10 452	181	Senegal	8 308	197	Chad	6 314	1 284
therlands	15 495	42	Yugoslavia	10 881	102	Burkina Faso	10 326	274	Austria	8 004	84	Tajikistan	6 102	143
dagascar	15 206	587	Angola	10 844	1 247	Belgium	10 140	31	Bolivia	7 900	1 099	Honduras	5 940	112
ria	14 614	185	Mali	10 700	1 240	Malawi	9 800	118	Rwanda	7 899	26	El Salvador	5 743	21
men	14 609	528	Guatemala	10 624	109	Zambia	9 500	753	Dominican Rep.	7 818	49	Israel	5 696	27
ile	14 271	757	Portugal	10 600	92	Somalia	9 180	638	Azerbaijan	7 559	87	Jordan	5 547	89
ry Coast	14 271	322	Greece	10 510	132	Niger	9 149	1 267	Switzerland	7 268	41	Georgia	5 448	27

North America

- North America is the third largest continent in the world, half the size of Asia. It stretches almost from the Equator to the North Pole.

- Three countries – Canada, the United States and Mexico – make up most of the continent. The state of Alaska is separated from the main lands of the United States.

- Greenland, the largest island in the world, is included within North America although it is a self-governing division of Denmark.

- In the east there are a series of large lakes. These are called the Great Lakes. A large waterfall called Niagara Falls is between Lake Erie and Lake Ontario. The St. Lawrence River connects the Great Lakes with the Atlantic Ocean.

- There are mountains, volcanoes and high plains in the west. Major rivers, mountains and lowlands are in the east.

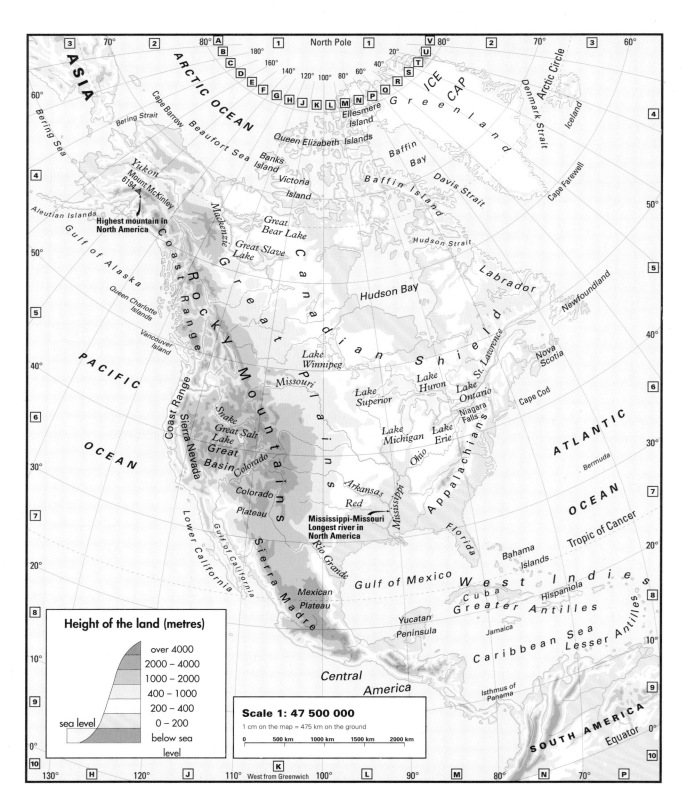

Height of the land (metres)

over 4000
2000 – 4000
1000 – 2000
400 – 1000
200 – 400
0 – 200
below sea level

sea level

Scale 1: 47 500 000

1 cm on the map = 475 km on the ground

0   500 km   1000 km   1500 km   2000 km

Largest countries – by area	Largest countries – by population	Largest cities
(thousand square kilometres)	(million people)	(million people)
Canada 9 976	United States 264	New York (USA) 16.3
United States 9 373	Mexico 93	Mexico City (MEXICO) 15.6
Mexico 1 958	Canada 30	Los Angeles (USA) 12.4
Greenland.....................342	Cuba 11	Chicago (USA) 7.6
Nicaragua 119	Guatemala 11	Philadelphia (USA) 4.9
Honduras 112	Dominican Republic 8	Toronto (CANADA) 4.3

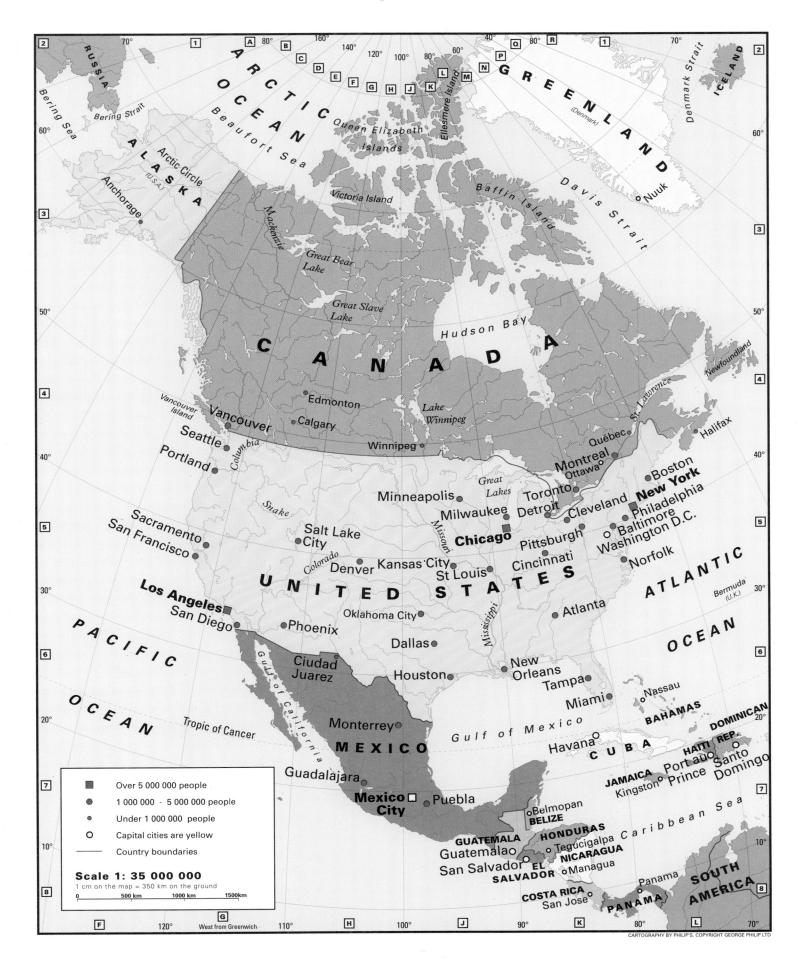

CARTOGRAPHY BY PHILIP'S. COPYRIGHT GEORGE PHILIP LTD

Canada – Physical

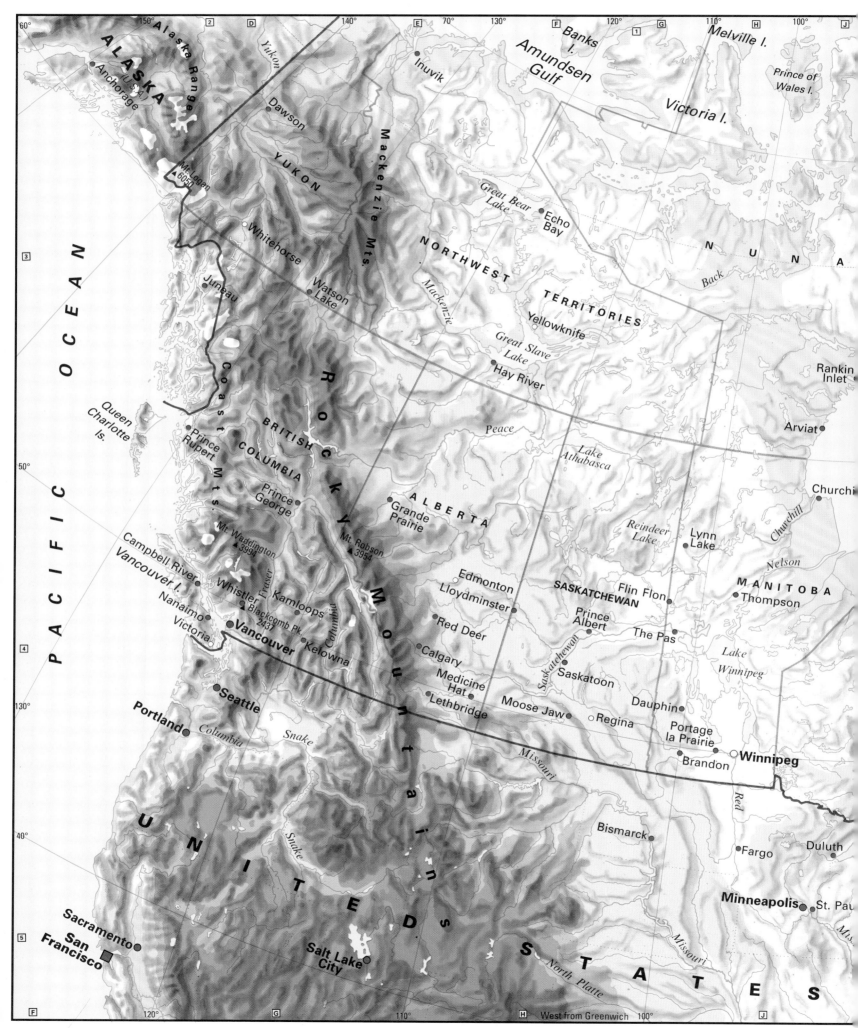

PACIFIC OCEAN

ALASKA (U.S.A.)
Anchorage
Alaska Range
Mt Logan ▲6050
Dawson
Yukon
YUKON
Whitehorse
Juneau
Watson Lake
Mackenzie Mts.

Queen Charlotte Is.
Prince Rupert
Coast Mts.
BRITISH COLUMBIA
Prince George
ROCKY
Mt. Waddington ▲3994
Mt. Robson ▲3954

Campbell River
Vancouver I.
Whistler
Fraser
Kamloops
Nanaimo
Victoria
Blackcomb Pk. 2437
Vancouver
Kelowna
Columbia

Seattle
Portland
Columbia
Snake

UNITED
Snake

Sacramento
San Francisco
Salt Lake City
North Platte

Inuvik
Banks I.
Amundsen Gulf
Melville I.
Prince of Wales I.
Victoria I.

Great Bear Lake
Echo Bay

NORTHWEST
TERRITORIES
Mackenzie
Yellowknife
Great Slave Lake
Hay River
Peace

NUNA

Back
Rankin Inlet
Arviat
Churchill

Lake Athabasca
Churchill

ALBERTA
Grande Prairie

Reindeer Lake
Lynn Lake
Nelson

MANITOBA
Thompson

Edmonton
Lloydminster
SASKATCHEWAN
Flin Flon

Red Deer
Prince Albert
The Pas

Calgary
Saskatchewan
Saskatoon
Lake Winnipeg

Medicine Hat
Lethbridge
Moose Jaw
Regina
Dauphin
Portage la Prairie

Mountains
Missouri
Brandon
Winnipeg
Red

Bismarck
Fargo
Duluth

STATES
Missouri
Minneapolis
St. Paul

West from Greenwich

18

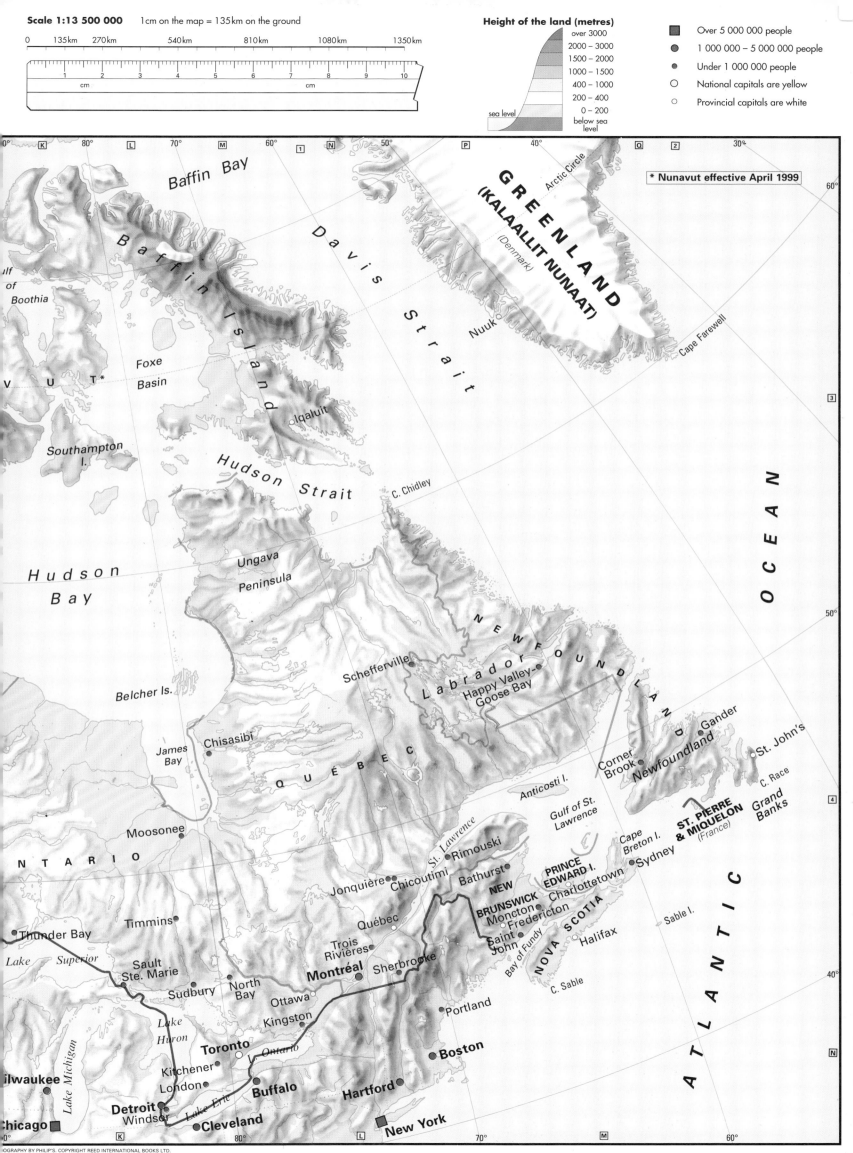

Scale 1:13 500 000   1cm on the map = 135km on the ground

0   135km 270km   540km   810km   1080km   1350km

cm   cm

Height of the land (metres)

over 3000
2000 – 3000
1500 – 2000
1000 – 1500
400 – 1000
200 – 400
sea level   0 – 200
below sea
level

Over 5 000 000 people
1 000 000 – 5 000 000 people
Under 1 000 000 people
National capitals are yellow
Provincial capitals are white

* Nunavut effective April 1999

Baffin Bay

Davis Strait

Gulf of Boothia

Baffin Island

Foxe Basin

GREENLAND
(KALAALLIT NUNAAT)
(Denmark)

Arctic Circle

Nuuk

Cape Farewell

Iqaluit

Southampton I.

V U N A V U T *

Hudson Strait

C. Chidley

Hudson Bay

Ungava Peninsula

NEWFOUNDLAND

Belcher Is.

Scheffferville

Labrador

Happy Valley-Goose Bay

James Bay

Chisasibi

QUÉBEC

Corner Brook

Gander

Newfoundland

St. John's

C. Race

Moosonee

Anticosti I.

Gulf of St. Lawrence

Grand Banks

ONTARIO

St. Lawrence

Rimouski

Cape Breton I.

ST. PIERRE & MIQUELON
(France)

Timmins

Jonquière Chicoutimi

Bathurst

NEW BRUNSWICK

PRINCE EDWARD I.

Charlottetown

Sydney

Sable I.

Thunder Bay

Québec

Moncton

Fredericton

NOVA SCOTIA

Halifax

Lake Superior

Sault Ste. Marie

Trois Rivières

Sherbrooke

Saint John

Bay of Fundy

Sudbury   North Bay

Montréal

C. Sable

40°

Lake Huron

Ottawa

Kingston

Portland

Lake Michigan

Toronto

L. Ontario

Boston

ATLANTIC

Milwaukee

Kitchener

London

Buffalo

Hartford

Lake Erie

Detroit

Windsor

Cleveland

New York

Chicago

OCEAN

Map labels:

ALASKA (USA)
Anchorage
Alaska Range
Mt. Logan ▲ 6050
Dawson
Yukon
YUKON
Whitehorse
Juneau
Watson Lake

Inuvik
Banks I.
Amundsen Gulf
Victoria I.
Melville I.
Prince of Wales I.
Great Bear Lake
Echo Bay
NORTHWEST
Mackenzie Mts.
Mackenzie
TERRITORIES
Yellowknife
Great Slave Lake
Hay River
N U N A
Back
Rankin Inlet
Arviat
Churchill

PACIFIC OCEAN

Queen Charlotte Is.
Prince Rupert
Coast Mts.
BRITISH COLUMBIA
Prince George
ROCKY
Mt. Waddington ▲ 3994
Campbell River
Vancouver I.
Whistler
Fraser
Kamloops
Blackcomb Pk. 2437
Nanaimo
Victoria
Vancouver
Kelowna
Columbia

Mt. Robson ▲ 3954
ALBERTA
Grande Prairie
Peace
Lake Athabasca
Reindeer Lake
Churchill
Lynn Lake
Nelson

Edmonton
Lloydminster
Red Deer
Calgary
Medicine Hat
Lethbridge
M O U N T A I N S

SASKATCHEWAN
Flin Flon
Prince Albert
Saskatchewan
Saskatoon
Moose Jaw
Regina
Dauphin
The Pas
Lake Winnipeg
MANITOBA
Thompson
Portage la Prairie
Brandon
Winnipeg

Seattle
Portland
Columbia
Snake
U N I T E D   S T A T E S
Snake
Missouri
Red
Bismarck
Fargo
Duluth
North Platte
Missouri
Minneapolis
St. Pa...

Sacramento
San Francisco
Salt Lake City

West from Greenwich

■ Over 5 000 000 people
● 1 000 000 – 5 000 000 people
● Under 1 000 000 people
○ National capitals are yellow
○ Provincial capitals are white

* Nunavut effective April 1999

Baffin Bay

Davis Strait

GREENLAND
(KALAALLIT NUNAAT)
(Denmark)

Arctic Circle

Nuuk

Cape Farewell

Gulf of Boothia

Baffin Island

N U N A V U T *

Foxe Basin

Southampton I.

Iqaluit

Hudson Strait

C. Chidley

Ungava Peninsula

Hudson Bay

Belcher Is.

James Bay

Chisasibi

QUÉBEC

Schefferville

Labrador

NEWFOUNDLAND

Happy Valley-Goose Bay

Corner Brook

Newfoundland

Gander

St. John's

C. Race

O C E A N

Moosonee

O N T A R I O

Anticosti I.

Gulf of St. Lawrence

Cape Breton I.

Sydney

ST. PIERRE & MIQUELON
(France)

Grand Banks

St. Lawrence

Rimouski

Jonquière Chicoutimi

Bathurst

PRINCE EDWARD I.

Charlottetown

Sable I.

Timmins

Québec

NEW BRUNSWICK

Moncton

Fredericton

NOVA SCOTIA

Halifax

Thunder Bay

Trois Rivières

Saint John

Lake Superior

Sault Ste. Marie

Sudbury

North Bay

Montréal

Sherbrooke

Bay of Fundy

C. Sable

Lake Huron

Ottawa

Kingston

Portland

A T L A N T I C

Toronto

L. Ontario

Lake Michigan

Kitchener

London

Buffalo

Hartford

Milwaukee

Detroit

Windsor

Lake Erie

Cleveland

Boston

Chicago

New York

TOGRAPHY BY PHILIP'S. COPYRIGHT REED INTERNATIONAL BOOKS LTD.

United States – Physical

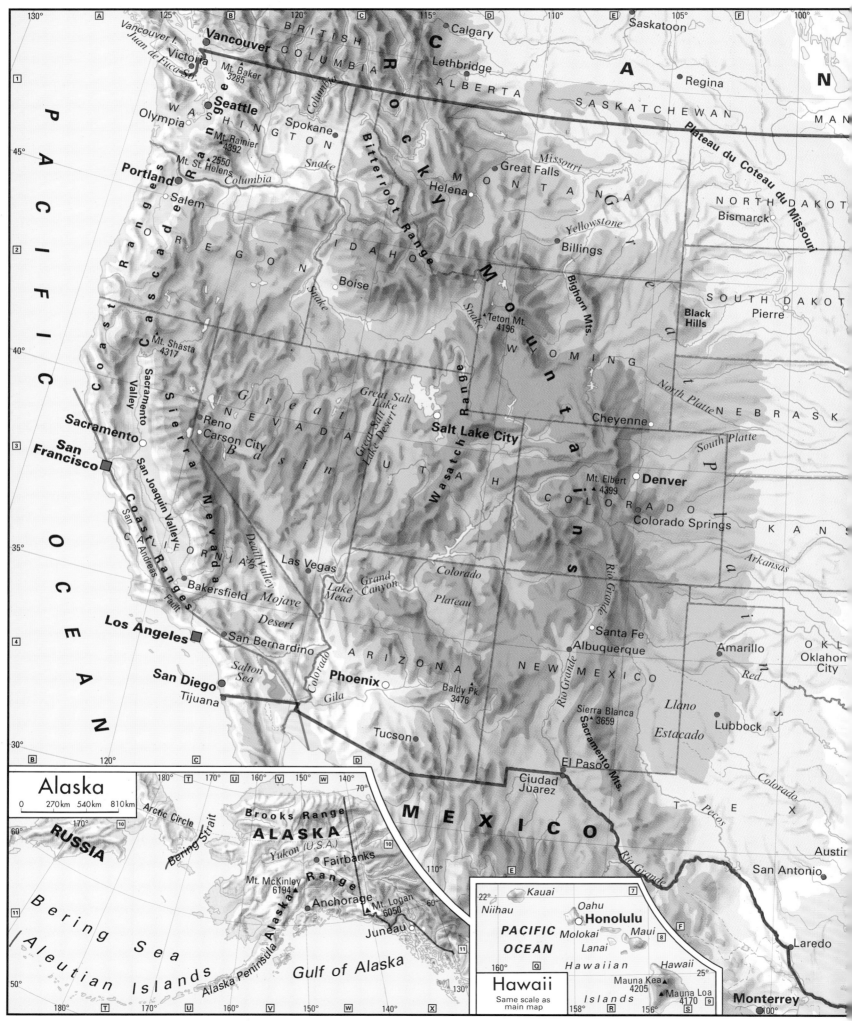

PACIFIC OCEAN

BRITISH COLUMBIA
Vancouver I.
Juan de Fuca Str.
Vancouver
Victoria
Mt. Baker 3285
Seattle
Olympia
WASHINGTON
Spokane
Mt. Rainier 4392
Mt. St. Helens 2550
Columbia
Portland
Salem
OREGON
Snake
Coast Range
Cascade Range
Mt. Shasta 4317
Sacramento
Sacramento Valley
San Francisco
Reno
Carson City
NEVADA
Great Basin
Sierra Nevada
San Joaquin Valley
San Andreas Fault
Coast Ranges
CALIFORNIA
Death Valley -86
Bakersfield
Las Vegas
Mojave Desert
Los Angeles
San Bernardino
Salton Sea
San Diego
Tijuana
Colorado
Gila
Phoenix
ARIZONA
Lake Mead
Grand Canyon
Colorado Plateau
Tucson

Calgary
Lethbridge
ALBERTA
ROCKY
Bitterroot Range
Great Falls
Helena
MONTANA
Missouri
Yellowstone
Billings
Bighorn Mts.
IDAHO
Boise
Snake
Teton Mt. 4196
WYOMING
MOUNTAINS
Great Salt Lake
Great Salt Lake Desert
Salt Lake City
UTAH
Wasatch Range
Mt. Elbert 4399
Denver
COLORADO
Colorado Springs
Colorado
Rio Grande
Santa Fe
Albuquerque
NEW MEXICO
Baldy Pk. 3476
Sierra Blanca 3659
Sacramento Mts.
El Paso
Ciudad Juarez
Rio Grande

Saskatoon
CANADA
Regina
SASKATCHEWAN
Plateau du Coteau du Missouri
MANITOBA
NORTH DAKOTA
Bismarck
Great Plains
SOUTH DAKOTA
Black Hills
Pierre
North Platte
NEBRASKA
Cheyenne
South Platte
Great Plains
KANSAS
Arkansas
Amarillo
OKLAHOMA
Oklahoma City
Red
Llano Estacado
Lubbock
TEXAS
Colorado
Pecos
Rio Grande
Austin
San Antonio
Laredo
Monterrey

MEXICO

Alaska

0   270km   540km   810km

Arctic Circle
RUSSIA
Bering Strait
Bering Sea
Aleutian Islands
Brooks Range
ALASKA
Yukon (U.S.A.)
Fairbanks
Mt. McKinley 6194
Alaska Range
Anchorage
Mt. Logan 6050
Juneau
Alaska Peninsula
Gulf of Alaska

Hawaii
Same scale as main map

PACIFIC OCEAN
Kauai
Niihau
Oahu
Honolulu
Molokai
Maui
Lanai
Hawaiian Islands
Hawaii
Mauna Kea 4205
Mauna Loa 4170

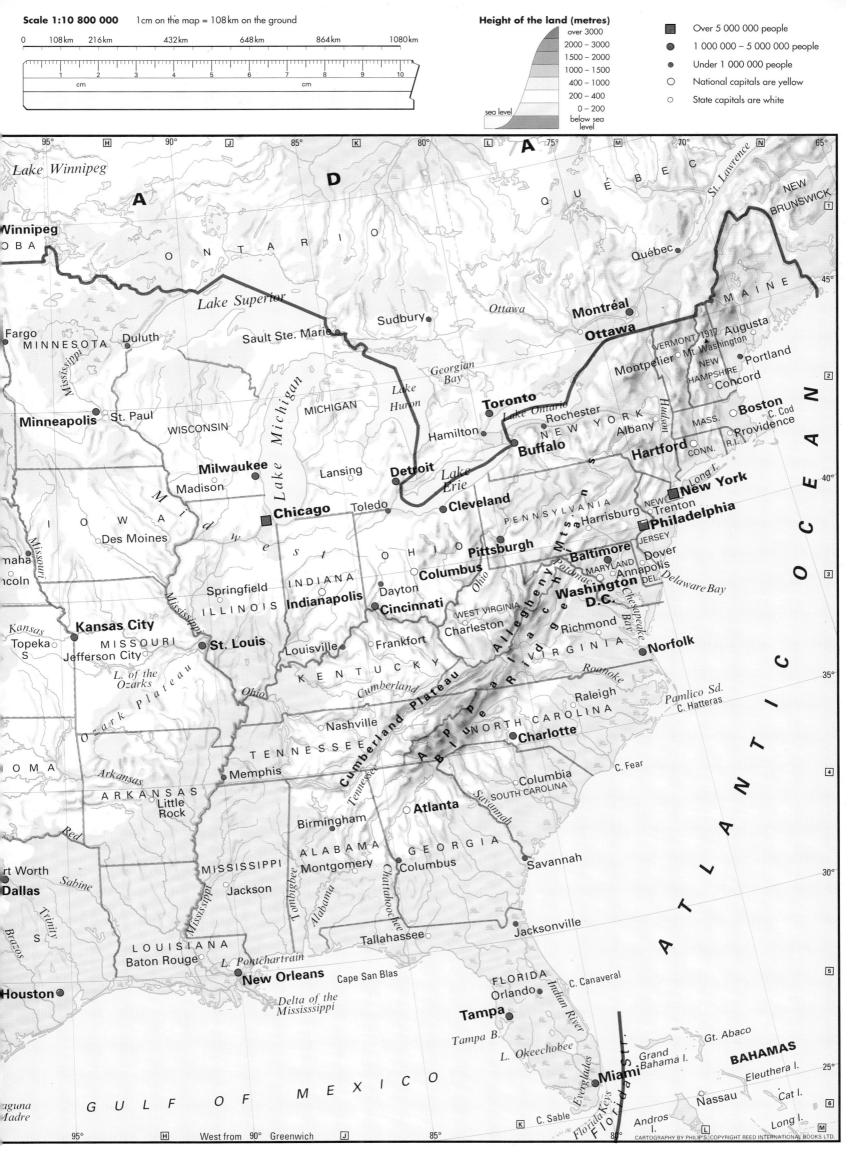

Height of the land (metres)

over 3000
2000 – 3000
1500 – 2000
1000 – 1500
400 – 1000
200 – 400
0 – 200
sea level
below sea level

■ Over 5 000 000 people
● 1 000 000 – 5 000 000 people
● Under 1 000 000 people
○ National capitals are yellow
○ State capitals are white

0   108km   216km   432km   648km   864km   1080km

CARTOGRAPHY BY PHILIP'S. COPYRIGHT REED INTERNATIONAL BOOKS LTD.

23

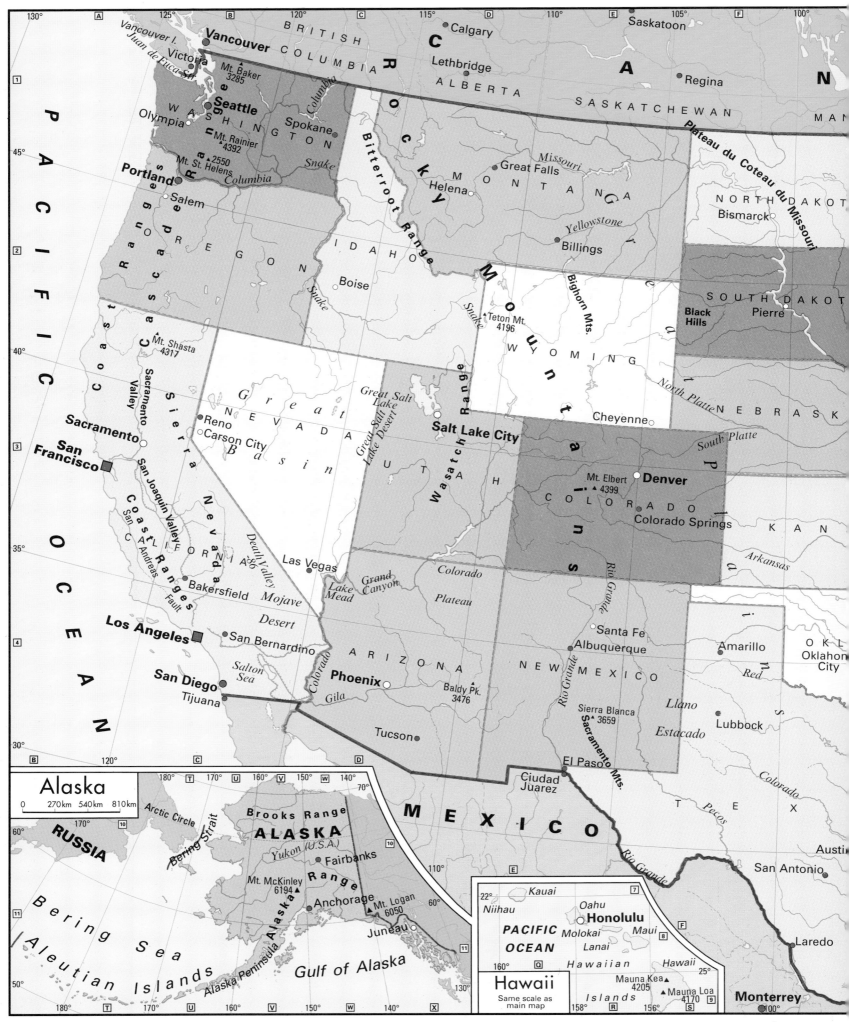

CANADA

BRITISH COLUMBIA
Calgary
Lethbridge
ALBERTA
Saskatoon
Regina
SASKATCHEWAN
MAN

Vancouver I.
Vancouver
Victoria
Juan de Fuca St.
Mt. Baker 3285
Seattle
Olympia
WASHINGTON
Spokane
Mt. Rainier 4392
Mt. St. Helens 2550
Columbia
Snake
Columbia

Portland
Salem
OREGON
Cascade Range
Coast Range

MONTANA
Great Falls
Helena
Missouri
Yellowstone
Billings
Bighorn Mts.

IDAHO
Boise
Snake
Bitterroot Range

ROCKY

Plateau du Coteau du Missouri
NORTH DAKOTA
Bismarck
SOUTH DAKOTA
Black Hills
Pierre

Mt. Shasta 4317
Sacramento Valley
Sierra Nevada
Reno
Carson City
NEVADA
Great
Basin
Great Salt Lake
Great Salt Lake Desert
Teton Mt. 4196
WYOMING
MOUNTAINS

Sacramento
San Francisco
San Joaquin Valley
Coast Ranges
CALIFORNIA
San Andreas Fault
Bakersfield
Death Valley -86

Las Vegas
Mojave
Desert
Lake Mead

Salt Lake City
Wasatch Range
UTAH
Grand Canyon
Colorado
Plateau

North Platte
NEBRASKA
Cheyenne
South Platte
Mt. Elbert 4399
Denver
COLORADO
Colorado Springs
Arkansas
KAN
Great
Plains

Los Angeles
San Bernardino
San Diego
Tijuana
Salton Sea
Colorado
Gila
Phoenix
ARIZONA
Baldy Pk. 3476
Tucson

Santa Fe
Albuquerque
Rio Grande
NEW MEXICO
Sierra Blanca 3659
Sacramento Mts.
El Paso
Ciudad Juarez

Amarillo
Red
Lubbock
Llano
Estacado
OKL
Oklahoma City
i
n
s

PACIFIC OCEAN

MEXICO
Rio Grande
TEX
Pecos
Colorado
Austin
San Antonio
Laredo
Monterrey

Alaska
0   270km 540km 810km

RUSSIA
Arctic Circle
Bering Strait
Brooks Range
ALASKA
ALASKA (U.S.A.)
Yukon
Fairbanks
Mt. McKinley 6194
Alaska Range
Anchorage
Mt. Logan 6050
Juneau
Bering Sea
Aleutian Islands
Alaska Peninsula
Gulf of Alaska

Hawaii
Same scale as main map

Kauai
Niihau
Oahu
Honolulu
Molokai
Maui
PACIFIC OCEAN
Lanai
Hawaiian
Hawaii
Mauna Kea 4205
Mauna Loa 4170
Islands

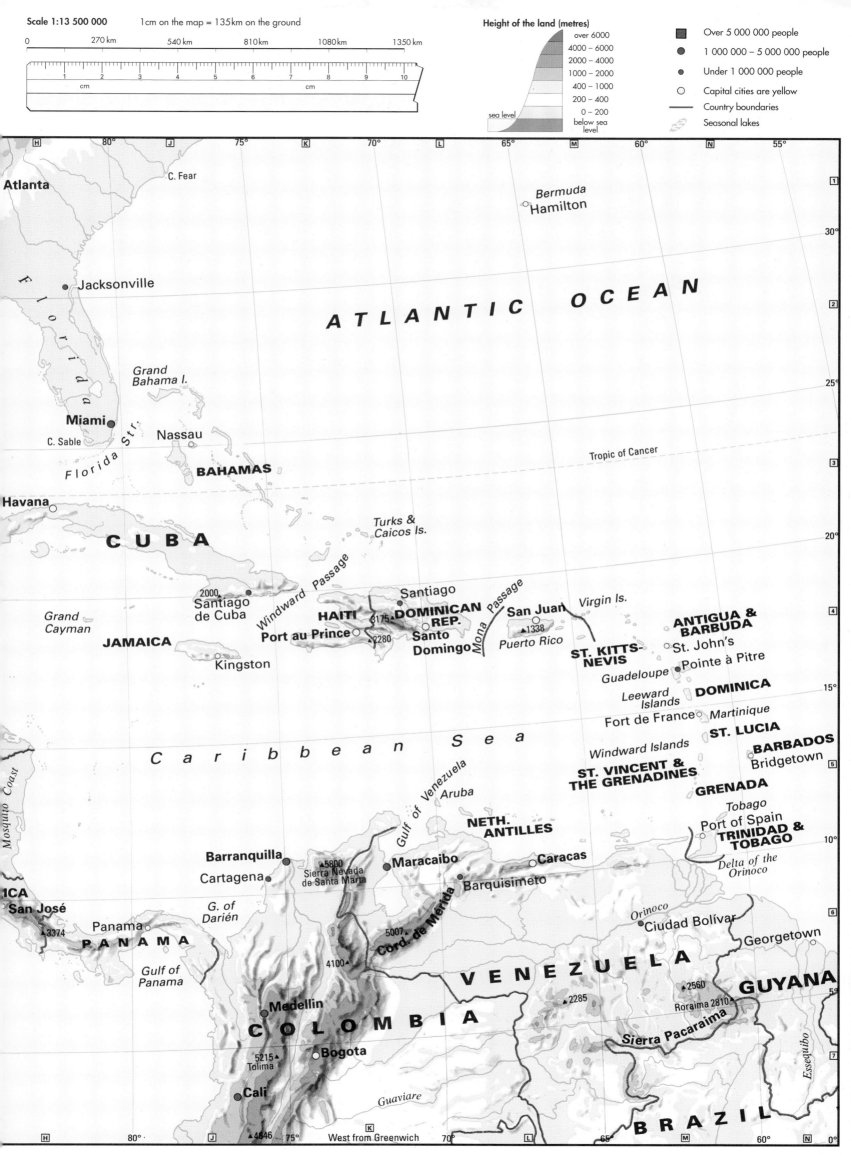

Height of the land (metres)

over 6000
4000 – 6000
2000 – 4000
1000 – 2000
400 – 1000
200 – 400
0 – 200
sea level
below sea level

Over 5 000 000 people
1 000 000 – 5 000 000 people
Under 1 000 000 people
Capital cities are yellow
Country boundaries
Seasonal lakes

Atlanta

C. Fear

Bermuda
○ Hamilton

A T L A N T I C   O C E A N

● Jacksonville

F l o r i d a

Grand
Bahama I.

Miami ●

C. Sable

Nassau ○

Tropic of Cancer

BAHAMAS

F l o r i d a   S t r.

Havana ○

C U B A

Turks &
Caicos Is.

2000. ●
Santiago
de Cuba

Grand
Cayman

JAMAICA

○ Kingston

W i n d w a r d   P a s s a g e

Santiago ●

HAITI
Port au Prince ○

▲3175
▲2280

DOMINICAN
REP.

Santo ○
Domingo

M o n a   P a s s a g e

San Juan ○

▲1338
Puerto Rico

Virgin Is.

ANTIGUA &
BARBUDA

○ St. John's

ST. KITTS-
NEVIS

Guadeloupe ● Pointe à Pitre

Leeward
Islands

DOMINICA

15°

Fort de France ○ Martinique

C a r i b b e a n   S e a

Windward Islands

ST. LUCIA

BARBADOS
Bridgetown ●

ST. VINCENT &
THE GRENADINES

GRENADA

Gulf of Venezuela

Aruba

NETH.
ANTILLES

Tobago
Port of Spain ○
TRINIDAD &
TOBAGO

M o s q u i t o   C o a s t

Barranquilla ●
Cartagena ●

▲5800
Sierra Nevada
de Santa Marta

Maracaibo ●

Caracas ○

Barquisimeto ●

Delta of the
Orinoco

ICA
San José ●

▲3374

PANAMA

G. of
Darién

Gulf of
Panama

5007 ▲
Cord. de Mérida

4100 ▲

V E N E Z U E L A

Orinoco
Ciudad Bolívar ●

Georgetown ○

● Medellin

C O L O M B I A

▲2285

Roraima 2810 ▲
▲2560

GUYANA

5215 ▲
Tolima

● Bogota ○

Sierra Pacaraima

E s s e q u i b o

● Cali

Guaviare

▲4646   75°   West from Greenwich   70°

B R A Z I L

South America

North America
Atlantic Ocean
Africa
Pacific Ocean
Antarctica

- The Amazon is the second longest river in the world. The Nile in Africa is the longest river, but more water flows from the Amazon into the ocean than from any other river.

- The range of mountains called the Andes runs for over 7,500 km from north to south on the western side of the continent. There are many volcanoes in the Andes.

- Lake Titicaca is the largest lake in the continent. It has an area of 8,200 sq km and is 3,800 metres above sea level.

- Spanish and Portuguese are the principal languages spoken in South America.

- Brazil is the largest country in area and population, and is the richest in the continent.

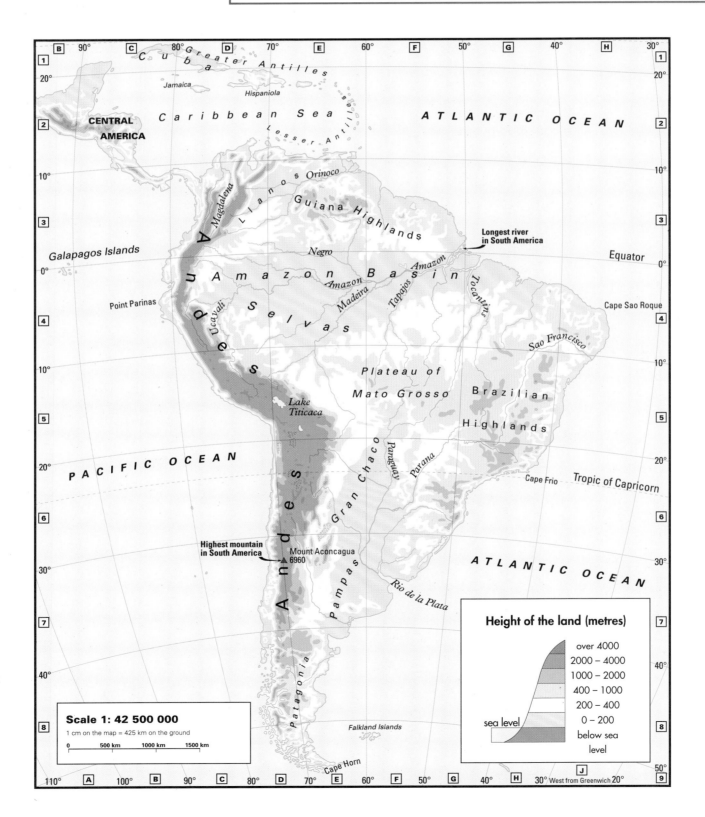

Scale 1: 42 500 000

1 cm on the map = 425 km on the ground

0   500 km   1000 km   1500 km

Height of the land (metres)

- over 4000
- 2000 – 4000
- 1000 – 2000
- 400 – 1000
- 200 – 400
- 0 – 200
- sea level
- below sea level

Largest countries – by area	Largest countries – by population	Largest cities
(thousand square kilometres)	(million people)	(million people)
Brazil....................8 512	Brazil....................161	Sao Paulo (BRAZIL)..............16.4
Argentina..............2 767	Colombia..............35	Buenos Aires (ARGENTINA).....11.0
Peru.....................1 285	Argentina..............35	Rio de Janeiro (BRAZIL)...........9.9
Bolivia..................1 099	Peru.....................24	Lima (PERU)......................6.6
Colombia...............1 139	Venezuela..............22	Bogota (COLOMBIA).................5.0
Venezuela..............912	Chile....................14	Santiago (CHILE)...................4.6

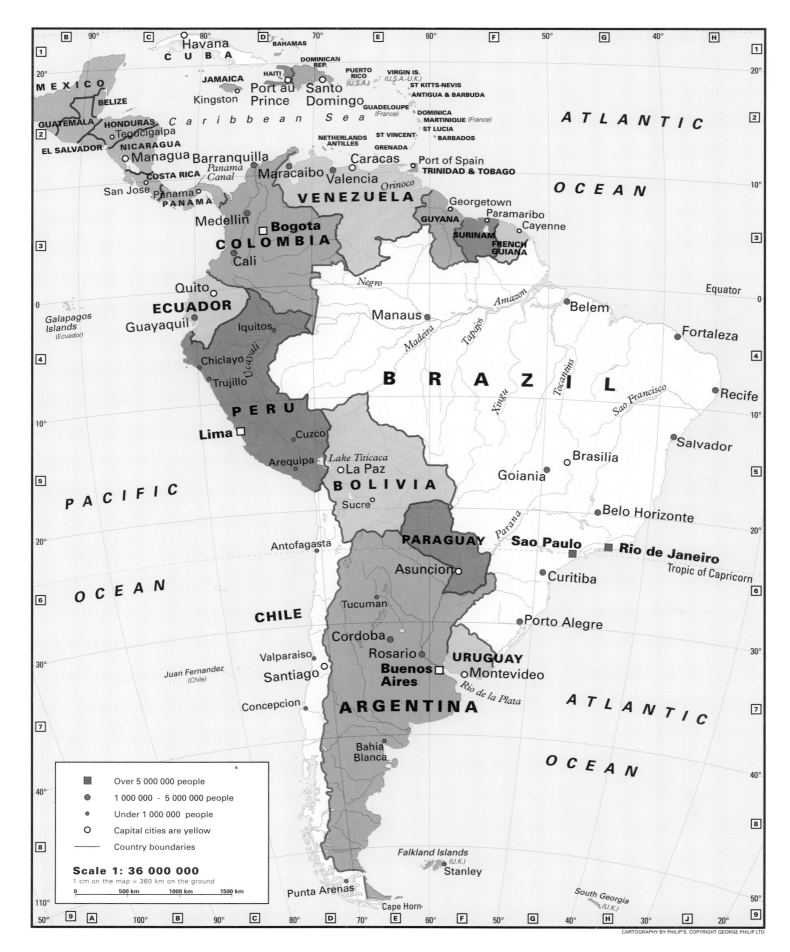

Australia and Oceania

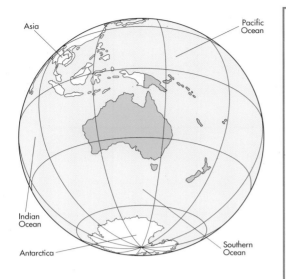

- The continent is often called Oceania. It is made up of the huge island of Australia, New Zealand and thousands of other islands in the Pacific Ocean

- Ayers Rock rises steeply out of the plains in central Australia. It is 348 metres high. The sides have deep gullies and unusual caves.

- There are thousands of islands in the Pacific. Some are volcanic mountains, while many others are low, flat coral islands.

- It is the smallest continent, only about a sixth the size of Asia.

- The Great Barrier Reef is the World's largest living thing. It is an area of coral over 2000 kilometres in length.

- The Pacific Ocean includes the deepest place in the World - the Mariana Trench is over 11,022 metres deep. It would take over half an hour for a steel ball weighing 0.5 kg to fall to the bottom.

- It is estimated that Australian aboriginals were living here for the past 40,000 years.

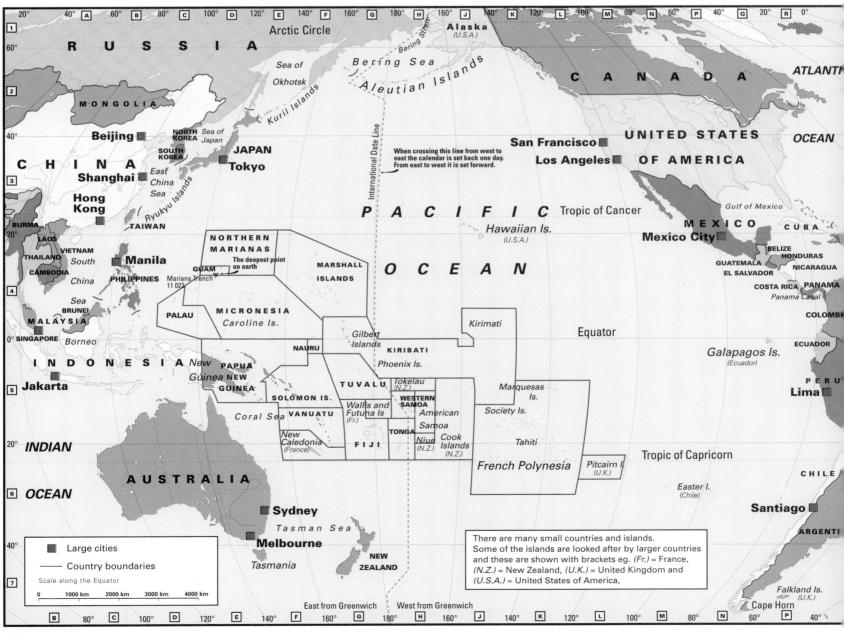

Largest countries – by area	Largest countries – by population	Largest cities
(thousand square kilometres)	(million people)	(million people)
Australia 7 684	Australia 18	Sydney (AUSTRALIA) 3.7
Papua New Guinea 462	Papua New Guinea 4	Melbourne (AUSTRALIA) 3.2
New Zealand 269	New Zealand 4	Brisbane (AUSTRALIA) 1.4
Solomon Islands 29	Fiji 0.8	Perth (AUSTRALIA) 1.2
New Caledonia 19	Solomon Islands 0.3	Adelaide (AUSTRALIA) 1.1
Fiji 18	New Caledonia 0.2	Auckland (NEW ZEALAND) 0.9

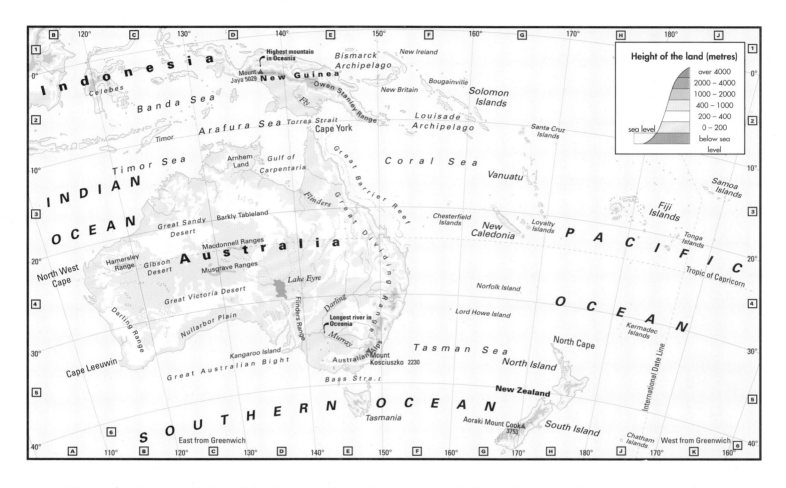

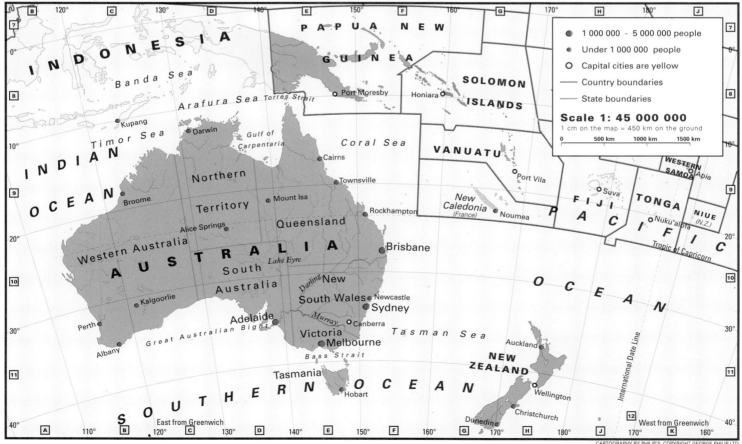

CARTOGRAPHY BY PHILIP'S. COPYRIGHT GEORGE PHILIP LTD

31

Africa

- ■ Africa is the second largest continent. Asia is the largest.

- ■ There are over 50 countries in Africa, some of them small in area and population. The population of Africa is growing more quickly than any other continent.

- ■ Parts of Africa have a dry, desert climate. Other parts are tropical.

- ■ The Sahara Desert is the largest desert in the world.

- ■ The highest mountains run from north to south on the eastern side of Africa. The Great Rift Valley is a volcanic valley that was formed 10 to 20 million years ago by a crack in the Earth's crust.

- ■ Mount Kenya and Mount Kilimanjaro are examples of old volcanoes in the area.

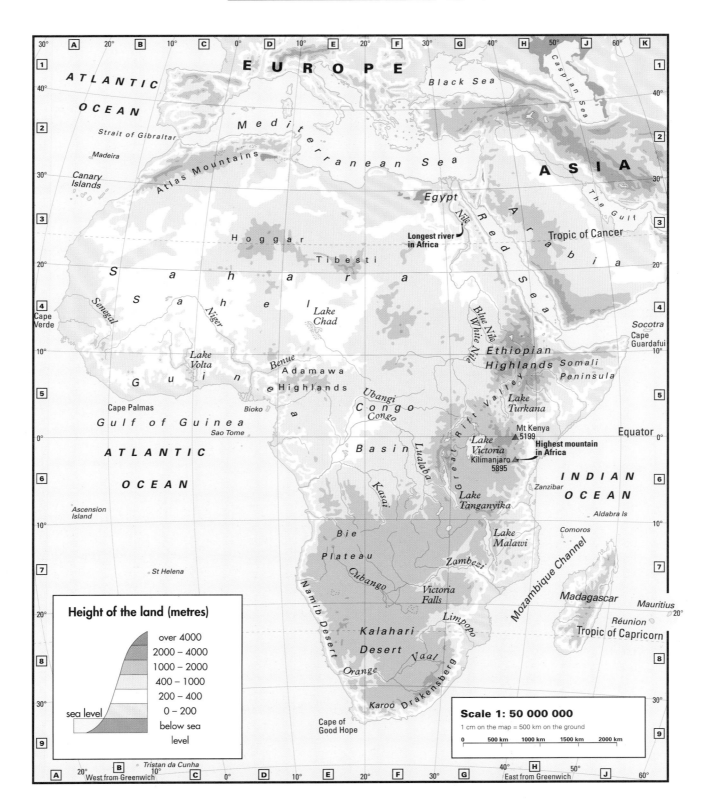

Height of the land (metres)

over 4000	
2000 – 4000	
1000 – 2000	
400 – 1000	
200 – 400	
0 – 200	
below sea level	

Scale 1: 50 000 000

1 cm on the map = 500 km on the ground

0   500 km   1000 km   1500 km   2000 km

Largest countries – by area	Largest countries – by population	Largest cities
(thousand square kilometres)	*(million people)*	*(million people)*
Sudan 2 506	Nigeria 89	Lagos (NIGERIA) 10.3
Algeria 2 382	Egypt 64	Cairo (EGYPT) 9.7
Congo (Dem. Rep. of) 2 345	Ethiopia 52	Kinshasa (DEM. REP. OF CONGO) ..3.8
Libya 1 760	Congo (Dem. Rep. of) 45	Alexandria (EGYPT) 3.4
Niger 1 267	South Africa 44	Casablanca (MOROCCO) 2.9
Chad 1 259	Tanzania 30	Abidjan (IVORY COAST) 2.5

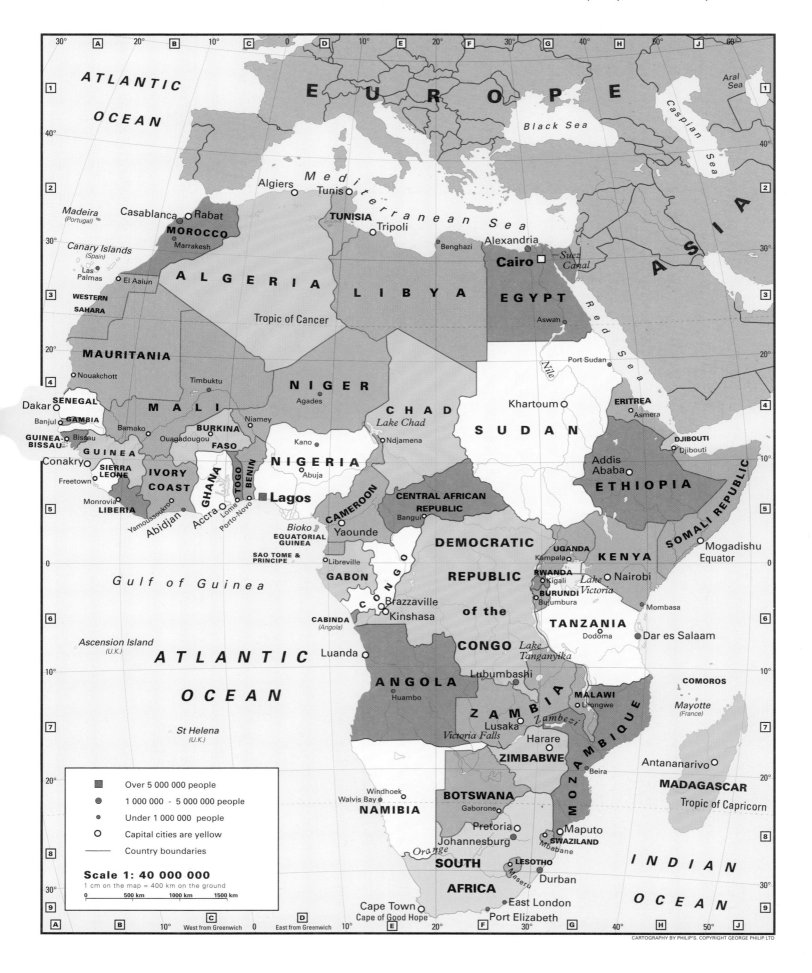

CARTOGRAPHY BY PHILIP'S. COPYRIGHT GEORGE PHILIP LTD

33

Europe

The European Union (formerly known as the European Community) was formed in 1993. The countries of Austria, Belgium, Denmark, Finland, France, Germany, Greece, Ireland, Italy, Luxembourg, the Netherlands, Portugal, Spain, Sweden and the United Kingdom are members. The European Union is a political and economic association that promotes a common currency and common trade markets.

- Europe is the second smallest continent. It is one fifth the size of Asia. Australia is slightly smaller than Europe.

- Great Britain is the largest island in Europe. Iceland is the second largest and Ireland is the third largest.

- Next to Asia, Europe is the most densely populated continent. Parts of Europe have 400 people per square kilometre.

- The great Northern European Plain stretches from the Atlantic Ocean to Russia. This plain has most of Europe's best farmland and many of its biggest cities.

- Europe is often refered to as the "peninsula of peninsulas". It forms the west end of Asia. At the same time, it has a very irregular coastline with a series of large and small peninsulas. As a result, most of Europe is within 480 kilometres of the Atlantic Ocean.

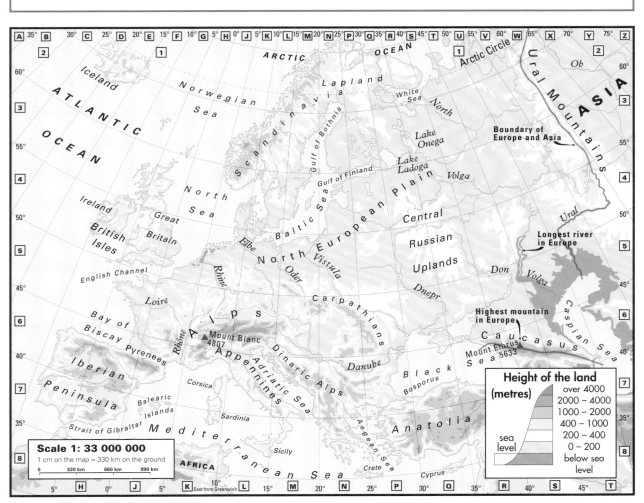

Scale 1: 33 000 000
1 cm on the map = 330 km on the ground
0   330 km   660 km   990 km

Height of the land (metres)
over 4000
2000 – 4000
1000 – 2000
400 – 1000
200 – 400
0 – 200
sea level
below sea level

Over 5 000 000 people
1 000 000 - 5 000 000 people
Under 1 000 000 people
Capital cities are yellow
Country boundaries

Scale 1: 18 000 000
1 cm on the map = 180 km on the ground
0   250 km   500 km   750 km

Largest countries – by area	Largest countries – by population	Largest cities
(thousand square kilometres)	(million people)	(million people)
Russia 17 075	Russia 148	Paris (FRANCE) 9.5
Ukraine 604	Germany 82	Moscow (RUSSIA) 9.2
France 552	United Kingdom 58	Istanbul (TURKEY) 7.3
Spain 505	France 58	London (UK)........................ 7.0
Sweden 450	Italy 57	St Petersburg (RUSSIA) 4.9
Finland 337	Ukraine 52	Madrid (SPAIN)...................... 3.0

CARTOGRAPHY BY PHILIP'S. COPYRIGHT GEORGE PHILIP LTD

Western Europe

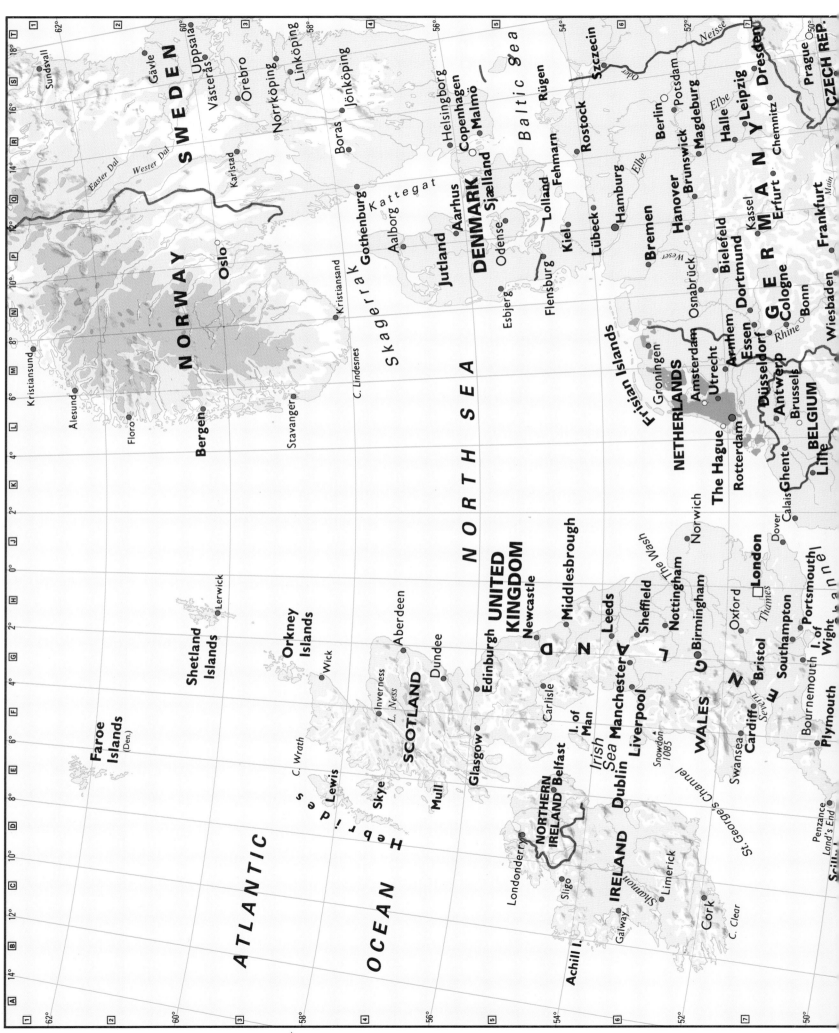

ATLANTIC OCEAN

NORTH SEA

Baltic Sea

SWEDEN
Sundsvall
Gävle
Uppsala
Västerås
Örebro
Norrköping
Linköping
Jönköping
Boras
Easter Dal
Wester Dal
Karlstad

NORWAY
Kristiansund
Ålesund
Floro
Bergen
Stavanger
Oslo
Kristiansand
C. Lindesnes

Skagerrak
Kattegat
Gothenburg
Helsingborg
Copenhagen
Malmö

DENMARK
Aalborg
Aarhus
Odense
Esbjerg
Flensburg
Jutland
Sjælland
Kiel
Lolland
Fehmarn

Helsingborg

Rügen
Rostock
Lübeck
Hamburg
Bremen
Hanover
Brunswick
Magdeburg
Halle
Leipzig
Dresden
Chemnitz
Erfurt
Frankfurt
Wiesbaden
Bonn
Cologne
Essen
Dortmund
Bielefeld
Kassel
Osnabrück
Düsseldorf
Arnhem
Antwerp

GERMANY
Szczecin
Berlin
Potsdam
Prague
CZECH REP.
Neisse
Oder
Elbe
Weser
Rhine
Main

Frisian Islands
Groningen
NETHERLANDS
Amsterdam
Utrecht
The Hague
Rotterdam
BELGIUM
Brussels
Ghent
Lille
Calais
Dover
Antwerp

UNITED KINGDOM
Newcastle
Middlesbrough
Leeds
Sheffield
Nottingham
Birmingham
Oxford
London
Thames
Norwich
The Wash
Portsmouth
I. of Wight
Bournemouth
Southampton
Bristol
Cardiff
Swansea
WALES
Snowdon 1085
Severn
Liverpool
Manchester
Irish Sea
I. of Man
Carlisle
Glasgow
Edinburgh
SCOTLAND
Inverness
L. Ness
Dundee
Aberdeen
Wick
C. Wrath
Hebrides
Lewis
Skye
Mull

Orkney Islands
Shetland Islands
Lerwick

Faroe Islands (Den.)

NORTHERN IRELAND
Belfast
Londonderry
IRELAND
Dublin
Sligo
Galway
Limerick
Shannon
Cork
C. Clear
Achill I.
St. George's Channel
Penzance
Land's End
Scilly Is.
Plymouth

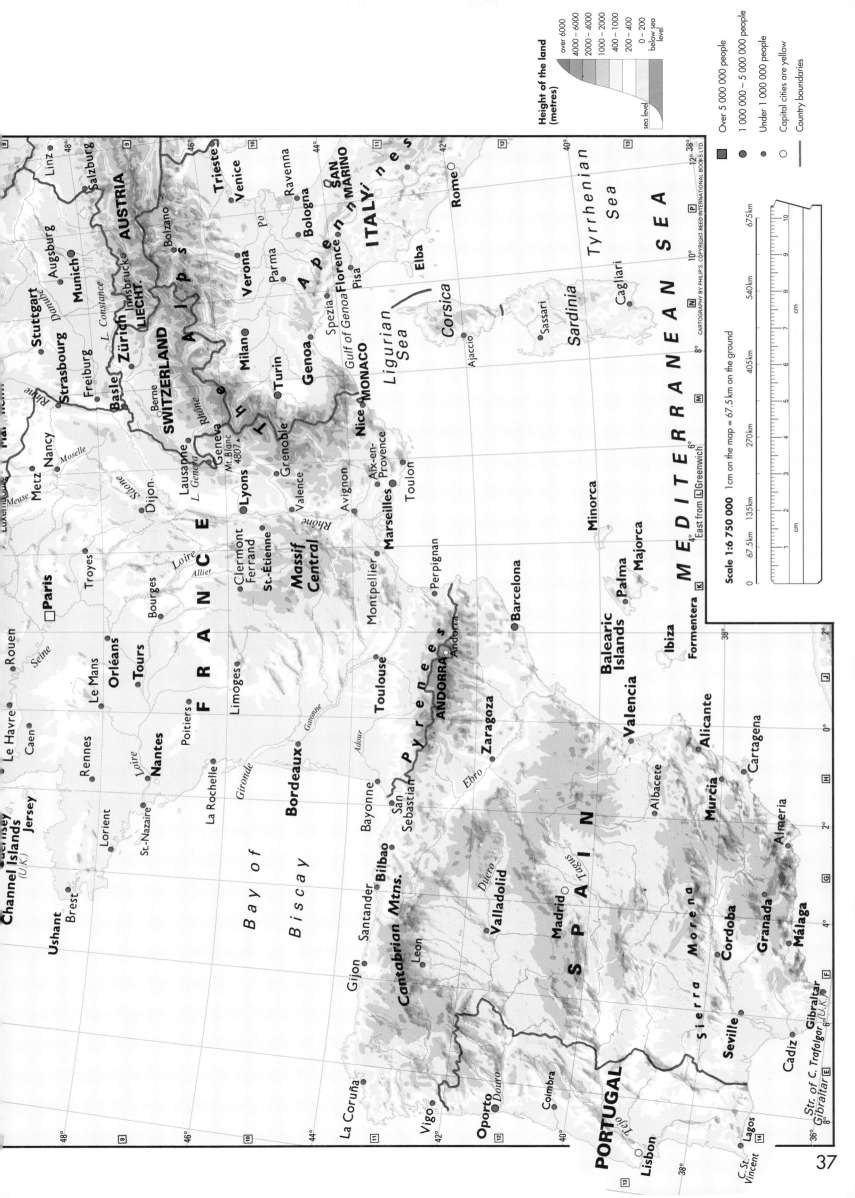

Southern Europe

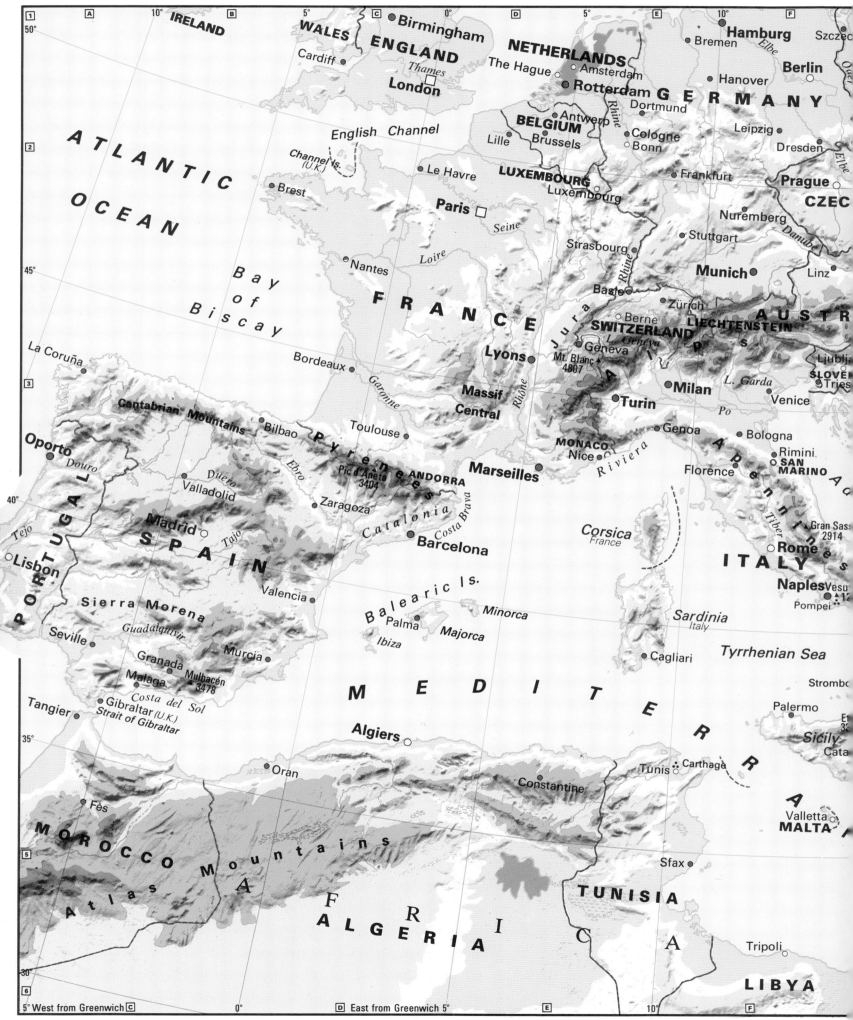

ATLANTIC
OCEAN

Bay
of
Biscay

IRELAND
WALES
ENGLAND
Birmingham
Cardiff
Thames
London
English Channel
Channel Is. (U.K.)
Brest
Le Havre
NETHERLANDS
The Hague
Amsterdam
Rotterdam
BELGIUM
Antwerp
Brussels
Lille
Bonn
Cologne
Dortmund
LUXEMBOURG
Luxembourg
Paris
Seine
Loire
Nantes
FRANCE
Strasbourg
Basle
Bordeaux
Garonne
Toulouse
Lyons
Rhône
Massif
Central
Mt. Blanc 4807
Geneva
L. Geneva
Berne
SWITZERLAND
Zürich
JURA
A
L
P
S
LIECHTENSTEIN
AUSTR
Milan
L. Garda
Venice
Turin
Po
MONACO
Nice
Genoa
Bologna
Rimini
SAN MARINO
Riviera
Florence
Tiber
APennines
Gran Sass 2914
Rome

GERMANY
Bremen
Hamburg
Szczec
Hanover
Berlin
Frankfurt
Leipzig
Dresden
Nuremberg
Stuttgart
Munich
Danube
Linz
Prague
CZEC
Ljubli
SLOVEN
Tries
Elbe
Rhine
Oder

La Coruña
Cantabrian Mountains
Bilbao
Oporto
Douro
Duero
Valladolid
PORTUGAL
Tejo
Lisbon
Madrid
Tajo
SPAIN
Zaragoza
Ebro
Pyrenees
Pic d'Anete 3404
ANDORRA
Catalonia
Costa Brava
Barcelona
Valencia
Murcia
Sierra Morena
Guadalquivir
Granada
Mulhacén 3478
Malaga
Seville
Costa del Sol
Gibraltar (U.K.)
Strait of Gibraltar
Tangier
Marseilles
Corsica
France
Sardinia
Italy
Naples
Vesu
Pompei
Tyrrhenian Sea
Cagliari
Stromb
Palermo
Sicily
Cata
Et 3

Balearic Is.
Minorca
Palma
Majorca
Ibiza
MEDITERRANEA

Algiers
Oran
Constantine
Tunis
Carthage
Valletta
MALTA

Fès
MOROCCO
Atlas Mountains
A
F
R
ALGERIA
I
C
A
TUNISIA
Sfax
Tripoli
LIBYA

5° West from Greenwich   0°   East from Greenwich 5°

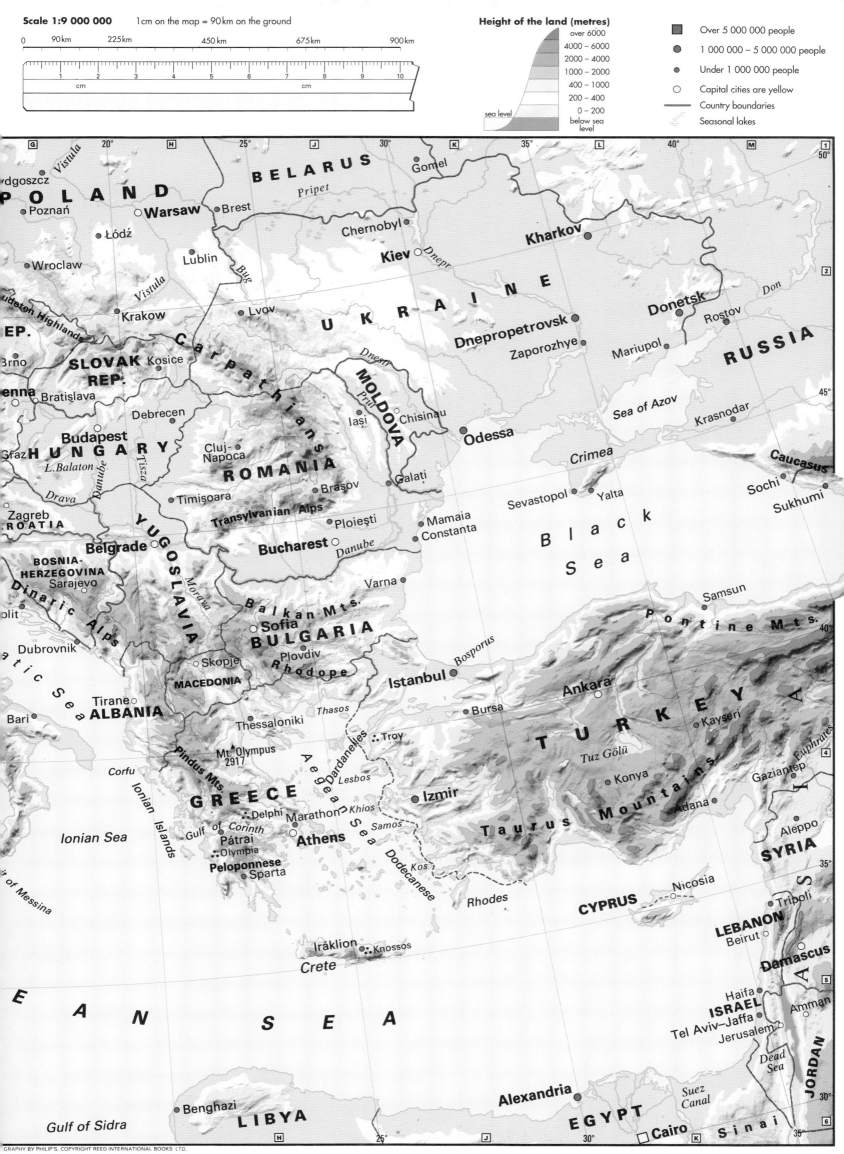

Scale 1:9 000 000   1cm on the map = 90km on the ground

0   90km   225km   450 km   675 km   900km

cm   1   2   3   4   5   6   7   8   9   10
           cm   cm

Height of the land (metres)

over 6000
4000 – 6000
2000 – 4000
1000 – 2000
400 – 1000
200 – 400
0 – 200
sea level   below sea level

Over 5 000 000 people
1 000 000 – 5 000 000 people
Under 1 000 000 people
Capital cities are yellow
Country boundaries
Seasonal lakes

G   20°   H   25°   J   30°   K   35°   L   40°   M   1   50°

Vistula
dgoszcz

BELARUS

POLAND
Poznań

Gomel

Pripet

Brest

Chernobyl

Łódź

Warsaw

Wroclaw

Lublin

Bug

Kiev

Dnepr

Kharkov

2

Vistula

Krakow

Lvov

U K R A I N E

Dnepropetrovsk

Donetsk

Rostov

Don

Brno

SLOVAK REP.

Kosice

Carpathians

Zaporozhye

Mariupol

RUSSIA

enna

Bratislava

Debrecen

MOLDOVA

Prut

Iaşi

Chisinau

Odessa

Sea of Azov

Krasnodar

45°

Budapest

HUNGARY

Cluj-Napoca

ROMANIA

Crimea

Sevastopol

Yalta

Sochi

Caucasus

Graz

L. Balaton

Tisza

Danube

Timişoara

Braşov

Galaţi

Sukhumi

Zagreb

Drava

ROATIA

YUGOSLAVIA

Transylvanian Alps

Ploieşti

Mamaia

Constanta

Black

olit

BOSNIA-HERZEGOVINA

Sarajevo

Belgrade

Morava

Bucharest

Danube

Sea

Samsun

3

Dinaric

Alps

Danube

Varna

Pontine Mts.

Dubrovnik

atic Sea

Balkan Mts.

Sofia

BULGARIA

Plovdiv

Bosporus

40°

Skopje

Rhodope

Istanbul

Ankara

MACEDONIA

Tirane

ALBANIA

Thessaloniki

Thasos

Troy

Bursa

T U R K E Y

Kayseri

Bari

Pindus Mts

Mt. Olympus
2917

Dardanelles

Lesbos

Tuz Gölü

4

Corfu

Aegean

Khios

Izmir

Taurus   Mountains

Gaziantep

Euphrates

Ionian Islands

GREECE

Delphi   Marathon

Sea

Samos

Konya

Adana

Ionian Sea

Gulf of Corinth

Pátrai

Athens

Samos

Dodecanese

Aleppo

Olympia

Peloponnese

Sparta

Kos

Nicosia

SYRIA

35°

t of Messina

Rhodes

CYPRUS

Tripoli

LEBANON

Beirut

Irāklion

Knossos

Damascus

Crete

Haifa

ISRAEL

Amman

Tel Aviv–Jaffa

Jerusalem

E   A   N   S   E   A

Dead Sea

JORDAN

30°

Benghazi

LIBYA

Alexandria

Suez Canal

EGYPT

Cairo

Sinai

35°

Gulf of Sidra

26°   H   28°   J   30°   K   32°

GRAPHY BY PHILIP'S. COPYRIGHT REED INTERNATIONAL BOOKS LTD.

39

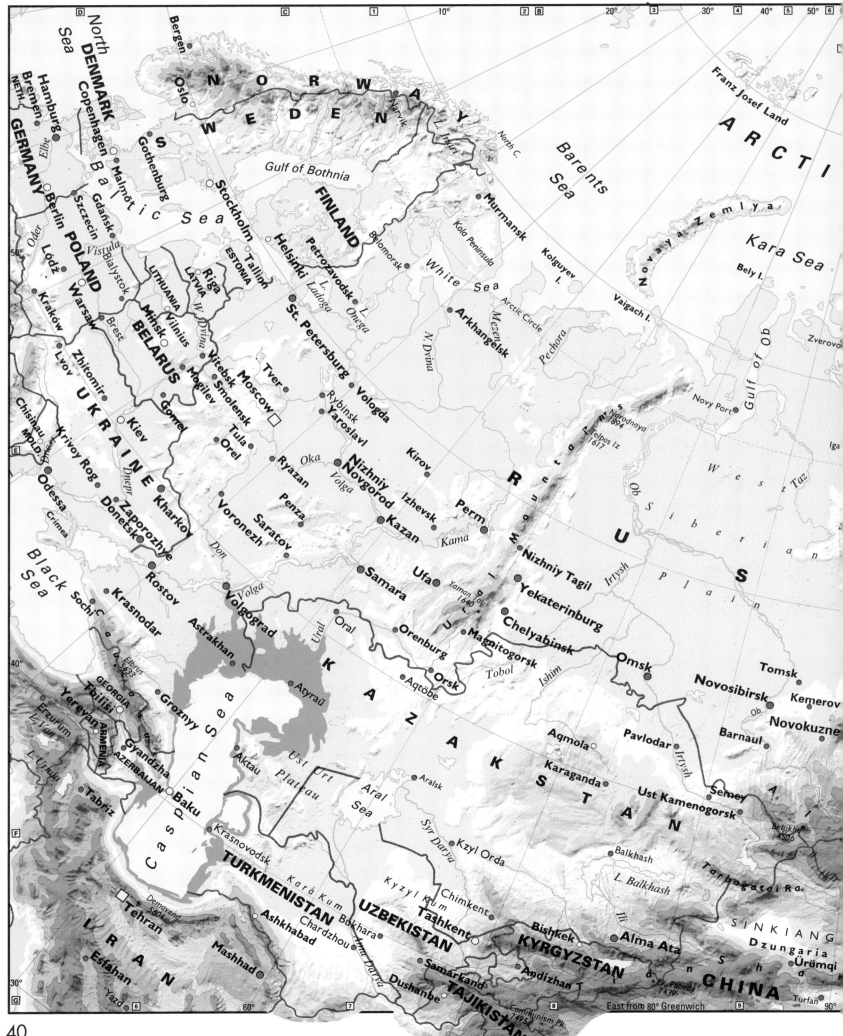

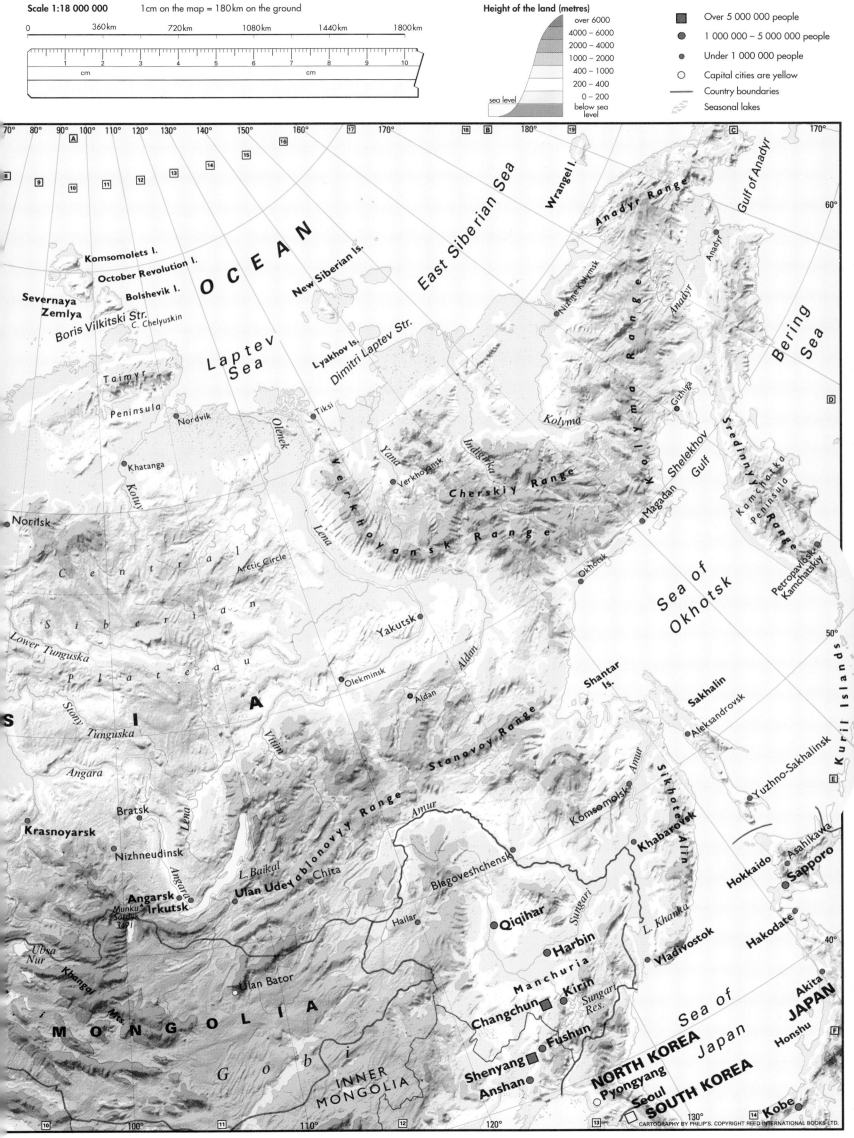

Height of the land (metres)

over 6000
4000 – 6000
2000 – 4000
1000 – 2000
400 – 1000
200 – 400
0 – 200
sea level
below sea level

Over 5 000 000 people
1 000 000 – 5 000 000 people
Under 1 000 000 people
Capital cities are yellow
Country boundaries
Seasonal lakes

0   360km   720km   1080km   1440km   1800km

cm   cm

OCEAN

Komsomolets I.
October Revolution I.
Bolshevik I.
Severnaya Zemlya
Boris Vilkitski Str.
C. Chelyuskin
Taimyr Peninsula
Nordvik
Khatanga

New Siberian Is.
Lyakhov Is.
Dimitri Laptev Str.

East Siberian Sea

Wrangel I.

Anadyr Range

Gulf of Anadyr

Anadyr

Laptev Sea

Olenek
Tiksi
Yana
Verkhoyansk
Indigirka
Cherskiy Range

Kolyma

Nizhne-Kolymsk

Gizhiga

Bering Sea

Norilsk

Lena
Arctic Circle

Verkhoyansk Range

Magadan   Shelekhov Gulf

Kamchatka Peninsula

Sredinnyy Range

Sea of Okhotsk

Petropavlovsk-Kamchatskiy

Central Siberian Plateau

RUSSIA

Yakutsk

Aldan

Stanovoy Range

Okhotsk

Shantar Is.

Sakhalin
Aleksandrovsk

Lower Tunguska

Stony Tunguska

Olekminsk
Aldan

Yuzhno-Sakhalinsk

Kuril Islands

Angara

Vitim

Amur

Komsomolsk

Sikhote Alin

Bratsk

Krasnoyarsk

Lena

Nizhneudinsk

L. Baikal

Blagoveshchensk

Amur

Sungari

Khabarovsk

Hokkaido
Asahikawa
Sapporo

Angara

Ulan Ude
Yablonovyy Range
Chita

L. Khanka

Angarsk
Irkutsk
Munku Sardyk 3491

Hailar

Qiqihar

Vladivostok

Hakodate

Ubsa Nur

Khangai

Mts.

Ulan Bator

Harbin

Akita
JAPAN

Manchuria
Kirin
Sungari Res.

Sea of Japan

MONGOLIA

Gobi

Changchun
Fushun

Shenyang

Honshu

INNER MONGOLIA

Anshan

NORTH KOREA
Pyongyang
Seoul
SOUTH KOREA

Kobe

CARTOGRAPHY BY PHILIP'S. COPYRIGHT REED INTERNATIONAL BOOKS LTD.

Asia

Arctic Ocean
North America
Europe
Pacific Ocean
Africa
Indian Ocean
Oceania

Asia extends from Europe in the West to the Pacific Ocean in the East. In the North, much of its shoreline lies within the polar regions of the Arctic Circle. In the South, Asia extends into the warm tropical areas at the equator. As a result, Asia includes many different climates and ecosystems.

■ Over 5 000 000 people
● 1 000 000 - 5 000 000 people
• Under 1 000 000 people
○ Capital cities are yellow
— Country boundaries

Scale 1: 42 000 000
1 cm on the map = 420 km on the ground
0   500 km   1000 km   1500 km

- ■ Asia is the largest continent. It is twice the size of North America.

- ■ It is a continent of long rivers and inland seas. Many of Asia's rivers are longer than Europe's longest rivers.

- ■ Asia contains well over half the world's population. The coastal areas of the south and east are the most crowded.

- ■ Seven of the top ten most populated countries in the world are in Asia: China, India, Indonesia, Russia, Japan, Pakistan and Bangladesh.

- ■ In Asia are found both the highest and lowest points on Earth. The shore of the Dead Sea is 395 metres below sea level. Mount Everest in the Himalayan Mountains is 8848 metres high.

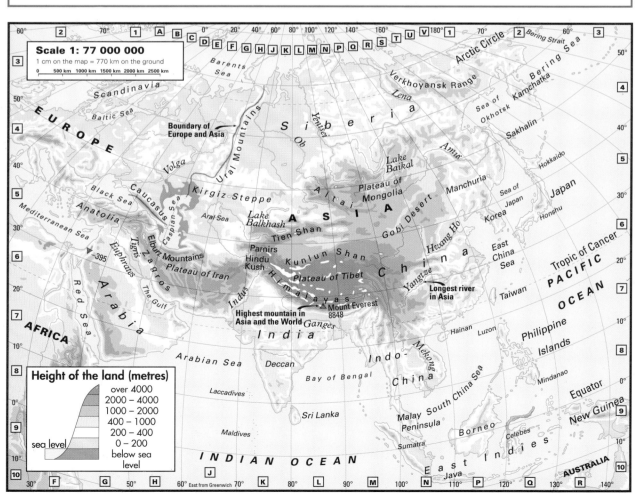

Scale 1: 77 000 000
1 cm on the map = 770 km on the ground
0   500 km 1000 km 1500 km 2000 km 2500 km

Height of the land (metres)
over 4000
2000 – 4000
1000 – 2000
400 – 1000
200 – 400
0 – 200
below sea level
sea level

Largest countries – by area	Largest countries – by population	Largest cities
(thousand square kilometres)	*(million people)*	*(million people)*
Russia.....................17 075	China..........................1 227	Tokyo (JAPAN).....................26.8
China.........................9 597	India..............................943	Bombay/Mumbai (INDIA).......15.1
India.........................3 288	Indonesia.......................199	Shanghai (CHINA)...............15.1
Kazakstan................2 717	Russia............................148	Beijing (CHINA)...................12.4
Saudi Arabia.............2 150	Pakistan.........................144	Calcutta/Kolkata (INDIA).....11.7
Indonesia.................1 905	Japan.............................118	Seoul (S. KOREA)................11.6

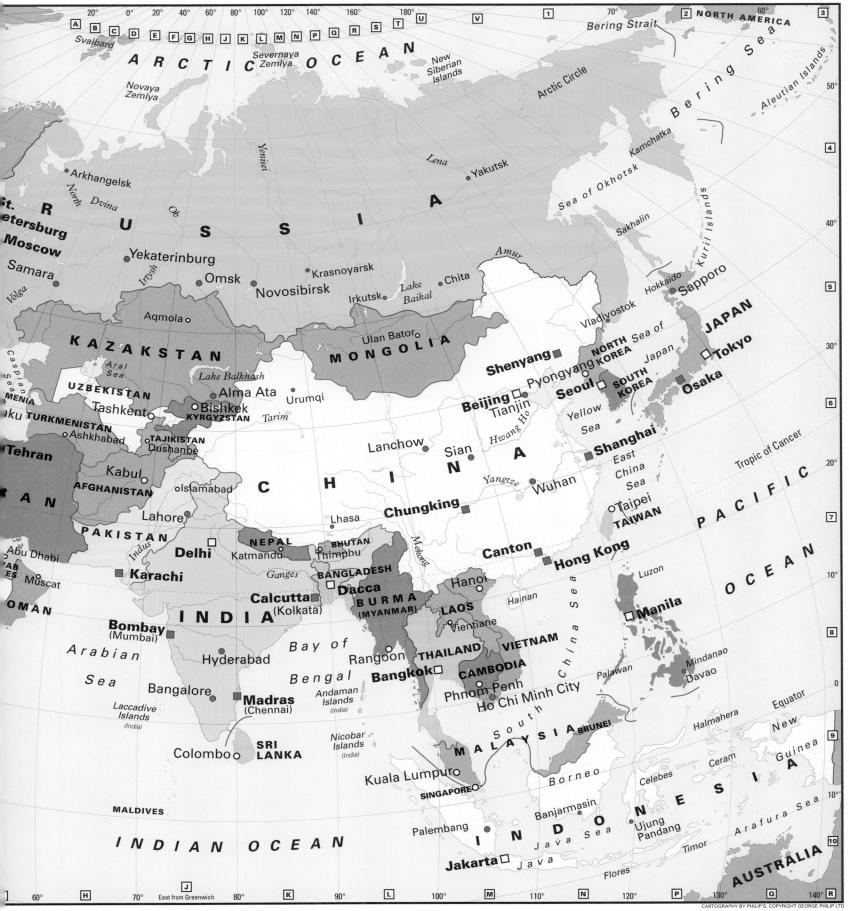

CARTOGRAPHY BY PHILIP'S. COPYRIGHT GEORGE PHILIP LTD

43

South Asia

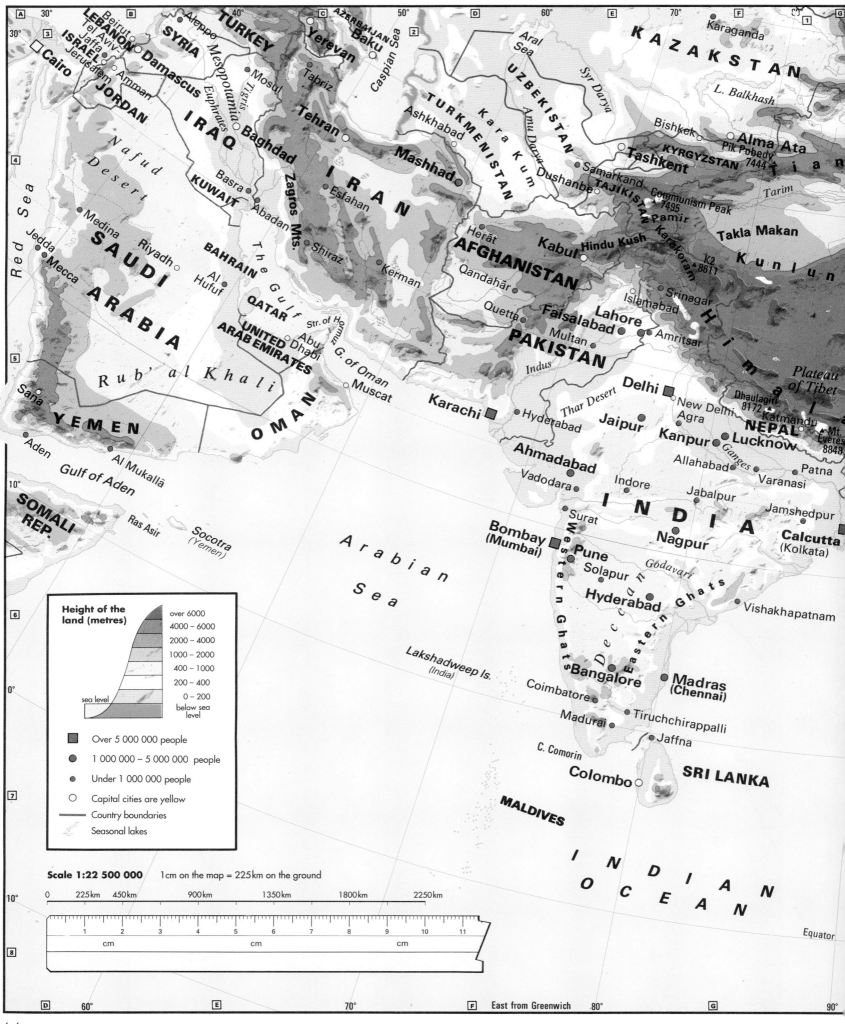

Height of the land (metres)

	over 6000
	4000 – 6000
	2000 – 4000
	1000 – 2000
	400 – 1000
	200 – 400
sea level	0 – 200
	below sea level

- ■ Over 5 000 000 people
- ● 1 000 000 – 5 000 000 people
- • Under 1 000 000 people
- ○ Capital cities are yellow
- — Country boundaries
- ⌇ Seasonal lakes

Scale 1:22 500 000   1cm on the map = 225km on the ground

0   225km   450km   900km   1350km   1800km   2250km

1   2   3   4   5   6   7   8   9   10   11
cm   cm   cm

East from Greenwich

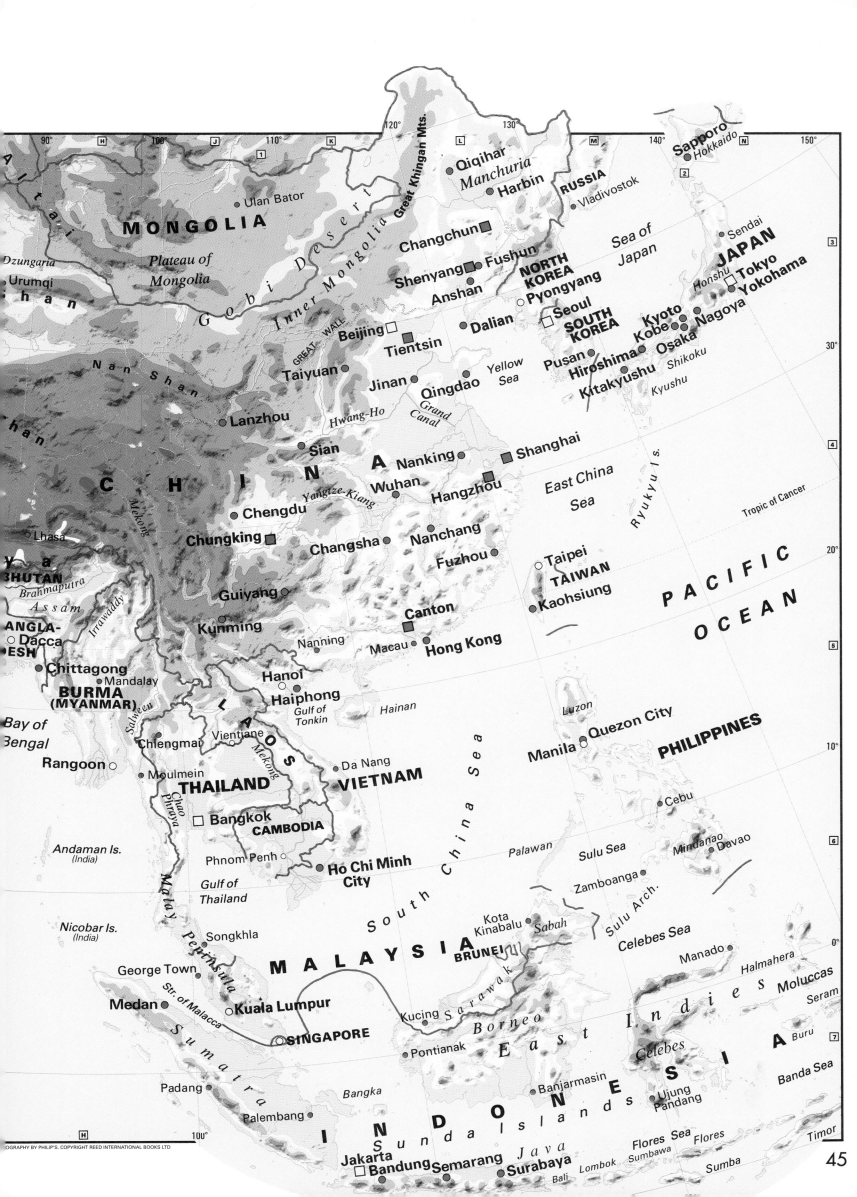

Altai

MONGOLIA

Dzungaria

Urumqi

Plateau of Mongolia

● Ulan Bator

Gobi Desert

Inner Mongolia   *Great Khingan Mts.*

● Qiqihar
Manchuria
● Harbin   **RUSSIA**

● Vladivostok

Nan Shan

Changchun ■

Shenyang ■ ● Fushun
● Anshan   **NORTH KOREA**
○ Pyongyang

● Sapporo
Hokkaido

Sea of Japan   **JAPAN**
● Sendai

Honshu   ● Tokyo
○ Seoul   **SOUTH KOREA**   Kyoto ● □ Yokohama

GREAT WALL

Beijing □
Tientsin ■
● Taiyuan

● Dalian

● Pusan   Kobe ● ● Osaka ● Nagoya
Hiroshima ●   Kitakyushu ●   *Shikoku*
Kyushu

● Lanzhou

● Jinan
● Qingdao

Yellow Sea

Hwang-Ho   *Grand Canal*

● Sian

C   H   I   N   A

Nanking ● ● Shanghai ■

East China Sea

Ryukyu Is.

Tropic of Cancer

● Chengdu

Wuhan ●   Hangzhou ■

Yangtze-Kiang

Lhasa ●

Mekong

● Chungking ■

Changsha ● ● Nanchang

● Fuzhou

○ Taipei
TAIWAN
● Kaohsiung

PACIFIC OCEAN

Y   a

BHUTAN
Brahmaputra
Assam

Irrawaddy

Guiyang ●

● Kunming

Nanning

Macau ● ● Hong Kong

ANGLA-
○ **Dacca**
ESH

● Chittagong
● Mandalay

Hanoi ○
Haiphong ○
Gulf of Tonkin

Hainan

Luzon
● Quezon City
Manila ○

PHILIPPINES

BURMA (MYANMAR)

Salween

● Chiengmai

Vientiane ○

L A O S

Mekong

● Da Nang

VIETNAM

Bay of Bengal

Rangoon ○
● Moulmein

THAILAND
Chao Phraya

□ Bangkok

CAMBODIA

● Cebu

● Mindanao ● Davao

● Zamboanga   *Sulu Arch.*

South China Sea

Andaman Is. (India)

Phnom Penh ○

● Ho Chi Minh City

Gulf of Thailand

Palawan   *Sulu Sea*

Celebes Sea

● Manado

Nicobar Is. (India)

● Songkhla

Malay Peninsula

Kota Kinabalu ●   *Sabah*

MALAYSIA   **BRUNEI**

East   I   n   d   i   e   s   Moluccas

Seram

● George Town

Str. of Malacca

● Medan

● **Kuala Lumpur**

Sarawak
Kucing ●   *Borneo*

Sumatra

○ **SINGAPORE**

Pontianak ●

Halmahera

● Banjarmasin

Celebes
● Ujung Pandang   *Buru*

● Padang
Bangka

I   N   D   O   N   E   S   I   A

● Palembang

Sunda   Islands

Java

Flores Sea   *Flores*

Timor

Jakarta ●
□ **Bandung**   Semarang ● ● Surabaya   *Bali*   *Lombok*   *Sumbawa*   *Sumba*

Banda Sea

Japan

Height of the land (metres)

- over 6000
- 4000 – 6000
- 2000 – 4000
- 1000 – 2000
- 400 – 1000
- 200 – 400
- 0 – 200
- below sea level

sea level

- Over 5 000 000 people
- 1 000 000 – 5 000 000 people
- Under 1 000 000 people
- Capital cities are yellow
- Country boundaries

Sungari

Kisi
Hengtaohotze
Mutankiang

CHINA

Dalnerechensk
Lesozavodsk
Ozero Khanka
Motashih
Spassk-Dalni
RUSSIA
Amgu

Ussuriysk
Dalnegorsk
Olga

Yenki
Vladivostok
Nakhodka

Changpai Shan
Musan
Tumen Ra.
Hyesan
Chongjin

NORTH KOREA
Songjin

Sikhote Alin

Sakhalin
Rebun
La Perouse Str.
C. Soya
Sea of Okhotsk
Riishiri
Wakkanai

Teshio
Asahi Dake 2290
Kitami
Ishikari B.
Asahikawa
Hokkaido
Otaru
Sapporo
Obihiro
Kushiro
Yubari
Uchiura B.
Muroran
C. Erimo

Okushiri
Hakodate
Str.
Matsumae
Tsugaru
Str.

Aomori
Hachinohe

Noshiro
Morioka
Akita

Yangyang
Kangnung

SOUTH KOREA
Pohang
Kyongju
Taegu
Ulsan
Masan
Pusan

Korea Strait
Tsushima
Str.
C. Hino
Hiroshima
Kure
Shimonoseki
Kitakyushu
Fukuoka
Tsushima
Sasebo
Kumamoto
Omuta
Nagasaki
Kyushu
Nobeoka

Sea of Japan

Ullung I.

Oki Is.
Kanazawa
Tottori
Okayama
Himeji
Sea
Takamatsu
Kobe
Okayama
Inland
Oita
Sea
Matsuyama
Shikoku
Kochi
Uwajima
C. Ashizuri
Bungo Channel
Tosa Bay

Sado
Niigata
Nagaoka
Toyama B.
Matsumoto
Fukui
Toyama
Gifu O
Ichinomiya
Kyoto
Osaka
Sakai
Yokkaichi
Wakayama
Kii Channel
C. Shiono
Nagoya
Ise B.
C. Daio

Sakata
Yamagata
Sendai
Fukushima
Koriyama
Iwaki
Utsunomiya
Nagano
Omiya
Tokyo
Chiba
Yokohama
Kawasaki
Yokosuka
Fujiyama 3776
Numazu
Shizuoka
Hamamatsu
Hitachi

Nii Is.
Miyake Is.
Miyake I.

Miyazaki
Miyakonojo
Kagoshima
Kagoshima B.
Osumi Channel
Tanega I.
Tokara Str.
Yaku I.
Tokara I.
Nakano I.
Akuseki I.

Hachijo I.
Aoga I.
Sumisu I.

PACIFIC OCEAN

East from Greenwich

Scale 1:6 750 000   1cm on the map = 67.5km on the ground

| 0 | 67.5km | 135km | 202.5km | 270km | 337.5km | 405km |

cm   cm

CARTOGRAPHY BY PHILIP'S. COPYRIGHT REED INTERNATIONAL BOOKS LTD

Polar Regions

The Polar regions are the areas around the North Pole and the South Pole. The area around the North Pole is known as the **Arctic** and is primarily an ice sheet floating on the Arctic Ocean. The area around the South Pole known as the **Antarctic**, a land mass, much of which is covered by ice 3000 metres thick in places, forming the continent of Antarctica. At the edges, chunks of ice break off to make icebergs. These float out to sea.

Since these regions are so far from the equator, the Arctic and the Antarctic receive sunlight for almost six months of the year. These two regions are among the coldest places on the Earth. The lowest temperature ever recorded on the Earth was in Antarctica (-89 C) in 1983.

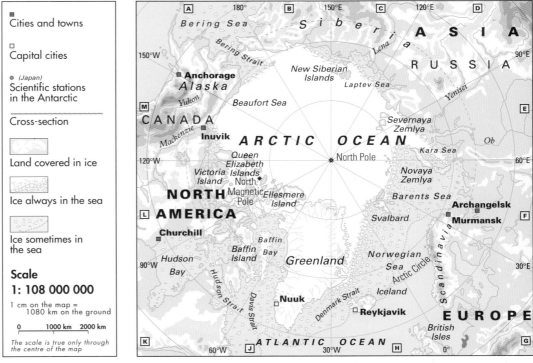

- Cities and towns
- Capital cities
- (Japan) Scientific stations in the Antarctic

Cross-section

Land covered in ice

Ice always in the sea

Ice sometimes in the sea

Scale
1: 108 000 000

1 cm on the map = 1080 km on the ground

0   1000 km   2000 km

The scale is true only through the centre of the map

Parts of North America, Asia and Northern Europe border on the Arctic Circle. In these areas, Aboriginal peoples have been able to uniquely use the environment to sustain a livelihood. The Arctic region is becoming important for its storehouse of minerals and development of these resources is beginning to have an impact upon the culture of these people.

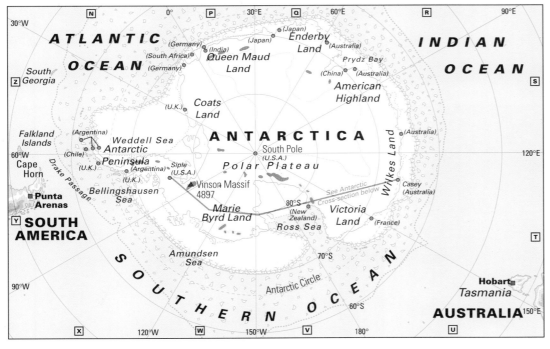

Antarctica has had no permanent settlement, although scientific research stations began to be established in the mid -1940s. The Antarctic Treaty, signed in 1959, was designed to preserve the uninhabited continent for peaceful purposes. The treaty bans military use, nuclear weapons, or disposal of radioactive waste. It also forbids any nations from making any claims on the continent.

Fishing, mainly for whales and krill, is carried out in the waters around the continent.

The diagram below shows a cross-section through Antarctica between two of the scientific research stations, Siple and Casey. It shows how thick the ice is on the ice sheets.

Cross-section of the Antarctic

2,000 m			East Antarctic Ice Sheet	2,000 m
1,000 m	Siple	ICE	Transantarctic Mountains	ICE	Casey	1,000 m
sea level	Bellingshausen Sea	West Antarctic Ice Sheet	Ross Ice Shelf		Indian Ocean sea level
-1,000 m					-1,000 m
-2,000 m		ROCK		ROCK	-2,000 m

1,000 km   2,000 km   3,000 km   4,000 km   5,000 km   6,000 km

Satellite Images

◄ **California, USA –** This image illustrates the diverse habitats that occur within a relatively small part of California around San Francisco Bay, due to the varied terrain and climate in this part of the USA. The Sierra Nevada mountains appear red in the top right, while the fertile Central Valley is a checkerboard between the mountains and the forested coast.

▼ **The Alps, Europe –** Europe's highest mountains appear white in this picture, and contrast with the deep glaciated valleys that weave between them.

▲ **Bangkok, Thailand –** You can see how this rapidly growing Asian city has expanded along the main roads leading outwards into the surrounding countryside.

◄ **The Nile Delta, Egypt –** The dependence of Egypt on the Nile River is clearly shown by this image of its delta. Almost all Egyptians live in the fertile green area.

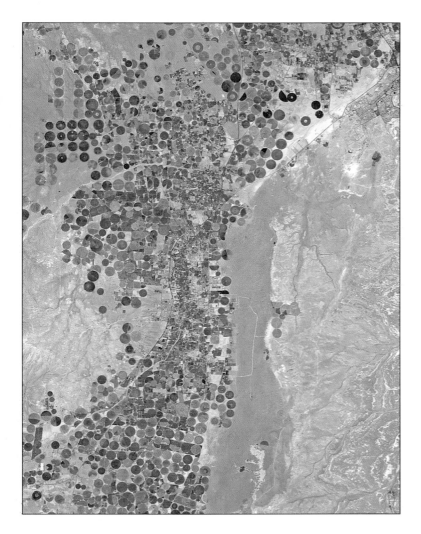

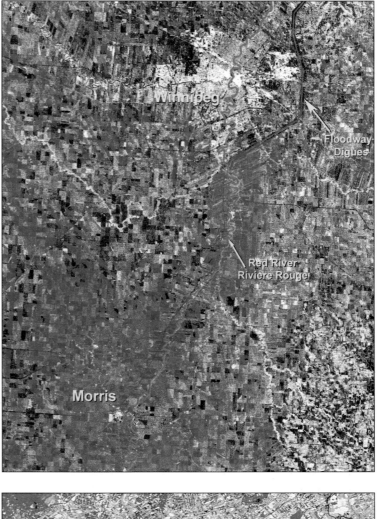

◀ **Irrigation in Saudi Arabia –** In desert areas, water is difficult to obtain and special technology is often needed to extract it from the ground. This is very expensive but oil-rich countries like Saudi Arabia have the resources to pay for the technology to develop their land. The red circles indicate irrigated agricultural land, and they contrast starkly with the barren desert.

▶ **Floods in Winnipeg, Canada –** In the late spring of 1997, record-breaking flooding on the Red River kept Canadian emergency response teams busy. Using remotely sensed images, like the one on the right, authorities were able to monitor the progress of the flooding from the US into Canada. The data obtained can now be used to improve flood prediction models.

▲ **The Great Lakes –** The five Great Lakes of North America are connected to the Atlantic Ocean by the St. Lawrence River, which leads into the Gulf of St. Lawrence at the top right of the image.

▲ **London, UK –** The centre of London is the dark green area towards the centre of the picture, with the West End to the left and the Isle of Dogs located between the large meander in the River Thames to the right.

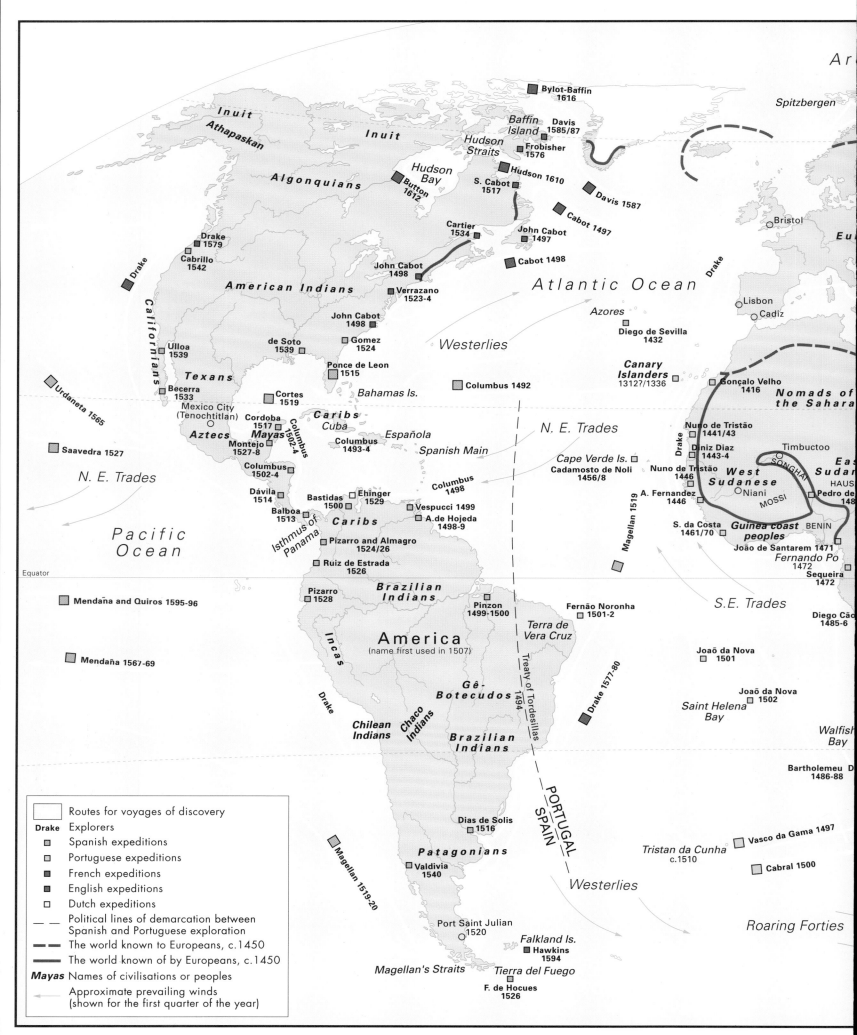

Bylot-Baffin 1616

Spitzbergen

Ar

Baffin Island
Davis 1585/87
Hudson Straits
Frobisher 1576
Hudson 1610
S. Cabot 1517
Davis 1587

Inuit

Athapaskan

Inuit

Hudson Bay
Button 1612

Cabot 1497

Bristol

Eu

Cartier 1534

John Cabot 1497

Cabot 1498

Drake

Drake 1579

Cabrillo 1542

John Cabot 1498

Verrazano 1523-4

Atlantic Ocean

Lisbon
Cadiz

American Indians

Azores

Drake

Californians

John Cabot 1498

Gomez 1524

Westerlies

Diego de Sevilla 1432

Ulloa 1539

de Soto 1539

Ponce de Leon 1515

Canary Islanders 1312?/1336

Gonçalo Velho 1416

Nomads of the Sahara

Texans

Becerra 1533

Bahamas Is.

Columbus 1492

Urdaneta 1565

Cortes 1519

Mexico City (Tenochtitlan)

Cordoba 1517

Caribs

Cuba

Españóla

N. E. Trades

Nuno de Tristão 1441/43

Timbuctoo

Aztecs

Mayas

Columbus 1502-4

Española

Columbus 1493-4

Spanish Main

Diniz Diaz 1443-4

SONGHAI

Ea
Sud

Saavedra 1527

Montejo 1527-8

Columbus 1502-4

Columbus 1498

Cape Verde Is.
Cadamosto de Noli 1456/8

Nuno de Tristão 1446

West Sudanese

Niani

HAUS

Drake

N. E. Trades

Dávila 1514

Bastidas 1500

Ehinger 1529

Vespucci 1499

Columbus 1498

A. Fernandez 1446

Pedro de
148

MOSSI

Balboa 1513

Caribs

A. de Hojeda 1498-9

Magellan 1519

S. da Costa 1461/70

Guinea coast peoples

BENIN

Pacific Ocean

Isthmus of Panama

Pizarro and Almagro 1524/26

João de Santarem 1471

Fernando Po 1472

Ruiz de Estrada 1526

Sequeira 1472

Equator

Pizarro 1528

Brazilian Indians

Pinzon 1499-1500

Fernão Noronha 1501-2

S.E. Trades

Diego Cão 1485-6

Mendaña and Quiros 1595-96

Terra de Vera Cruz

America
(name first used in 1507)

João da Nova 1501

Incas

Mendaña 1567-69

Gê-Botecudos

Treaty of Tordesillas 1494

João da Nova 1502

Saint Helena Bay

Drake

Chilean Indians

Chaco Indians

Brazilian Indians

Drake 1577-80

Walfis
Bay

Bartholemeu D
1486-88

Dias de Solis 1516

PORTUGAL
SPAIN

Tristan da Cunha c.1510

Vasco da Gama 1497

Magellan 1519-20

Patagonians

Valdivia 1540

Cabral 1500

Westerlies

Port Saint Julian 1520

Falkland Is.
Hawkins 1594

Roaring Forties

Magellan's Straits

Tierra del Fuego

F. de Hocues 1526

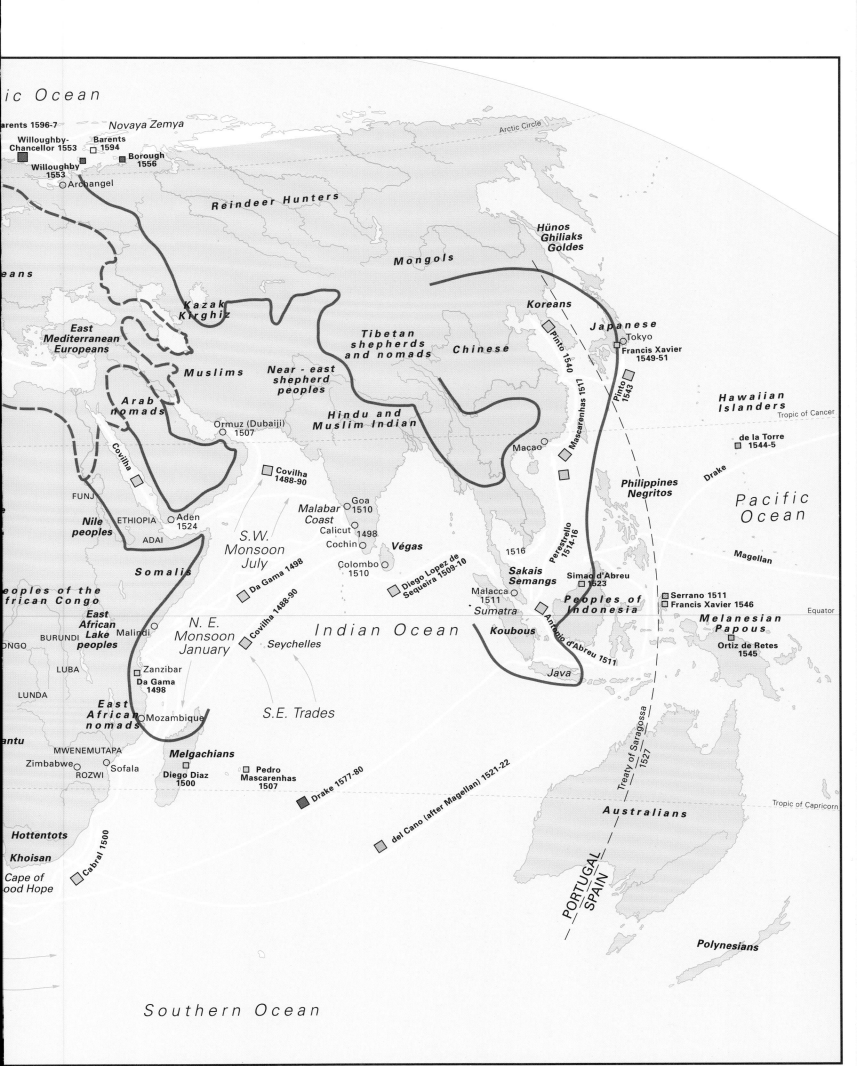

ic Ocean

arents 1596-7
Novaya Zemya
Willoughby-
Chancellor 1553
Barents
1594
Borough
1556
Willoughby
1553
Archangel

Reindeer Hunters

Mongols

Hünos
Ghiliaks
Goldes

Koreans

Japanese

eans

Kazak
Kirghiz

Pinto 1540

Tokyo
Francis Xavier
1549-51

East
Mediterranean
Europeans

Muslims

Tibetan
shepherds
and nomads

Chinese

Near-east
shepherd
peoples

Pinto
1543

Arab
nomads

Covilha

Ormuz (Dubaiji)
1507

Hindu and
Muslim Indian

Hawaiian
Islanders
Tropic of Cancer

de la Torre
1544-5

Macao

Drake

FUNJ

Aden
1524

Covilha
1488-90

Goa
1510

Philippines
Negritos

Pacific
Ocean

Nile
peoples

ETHIOPIA

Malabar
Coast
Calicut 1498
Cochin

ADAI

Somalis

S.W.
Monsoon
July

Végas

1516

Magellan

Colombo
1510

Da Gama 1498

Diego Lopez de
Sequeira 1509-10

Sakais
Semangs

Simao d'Abreu
1523

eoples of the
frican Congo

East
African
Lake
peoples

Malindi

BURUNDI

N. E.
Monsoon
January

Covilha 1488-90

Seychelles

Malacca
1511

Peoples of
Indonesia

Serrano 1511
Francis Xavier 1546

Equator

ONGO

Sumatra

Koubous

Antonio d'Abreu 1511

Melanesian
Papous

Ortiz de Retes
1545

LUBA

Zanzibar
Da Gama
1498

Indian Ocean

Java

LUNDA

East
African
nomads

Mozambique

S.E. Trades

MWENEMUTAPA

Melgachians

Zimbabwe
Sofala

ROZWI

Diego Diaz
1500

Pedro
Mascarenhas
1507

Drake 1577-80

Australians

Tropic of Capricorn

Hottentots

Khoisan

Cabral 1500

del Cano (after Magellan) 1521-22

Cape of
ood Hope

Southern Ocean

Polynesians

PORTUGAL
SPAIN

CARTOGRAPHY BY PHILIP'S. COPYRIGHT GEORGE PHILIP LTD

51

Time Zones

12midnight   2AM   4AM   6AM   8AM   10AM

AM Behind

PM | AM

lose one calendar day

Monday
Sunday

International Date Line

ALASKAN
TIME
Anchorage

MOUNTAIN

PACIFIC
Vancouver

CENTRAL

ATLANTIC
TIME

EASTERN
Montreal

3:30

London

TIME
Denver

Chicago

Madrid
Lisbon

TIME
San Francisco

TIME
Dallas

TIME
New York

Los Angeles

TIME
Atlanta

Honolulu

Miami

Mexico City

San Juan

Panama
City
Caracas

Dakar

Bogota

3:30

Abidjan

9:30

Lima

Tahiti

Rio de Janeiro

Santiago

Auckland

Buenos Aires

12:45

add one calendar day

Projection: *Mercator*

Note: Certain of the time zones are affected by the incidence of "Summer Time" in countries where it is adopted.

Zones using Greenwich Mean Time

Zones behind Greenwich Mean Time

Half hour zones

Zones ahead of Greenwich Mean Time

The Earth rotates through 360° in 24 hours, and so moves 15° every hour. The World is divided into 24 standard time zones, each centred on lines of longitude at 15° intervals. The Greenwich meridian lies on the centre of the first zone. All places to the west of Greenwich are one hour behind for every 15° of longitude; places to the east are ahead by one hour for every 15°.

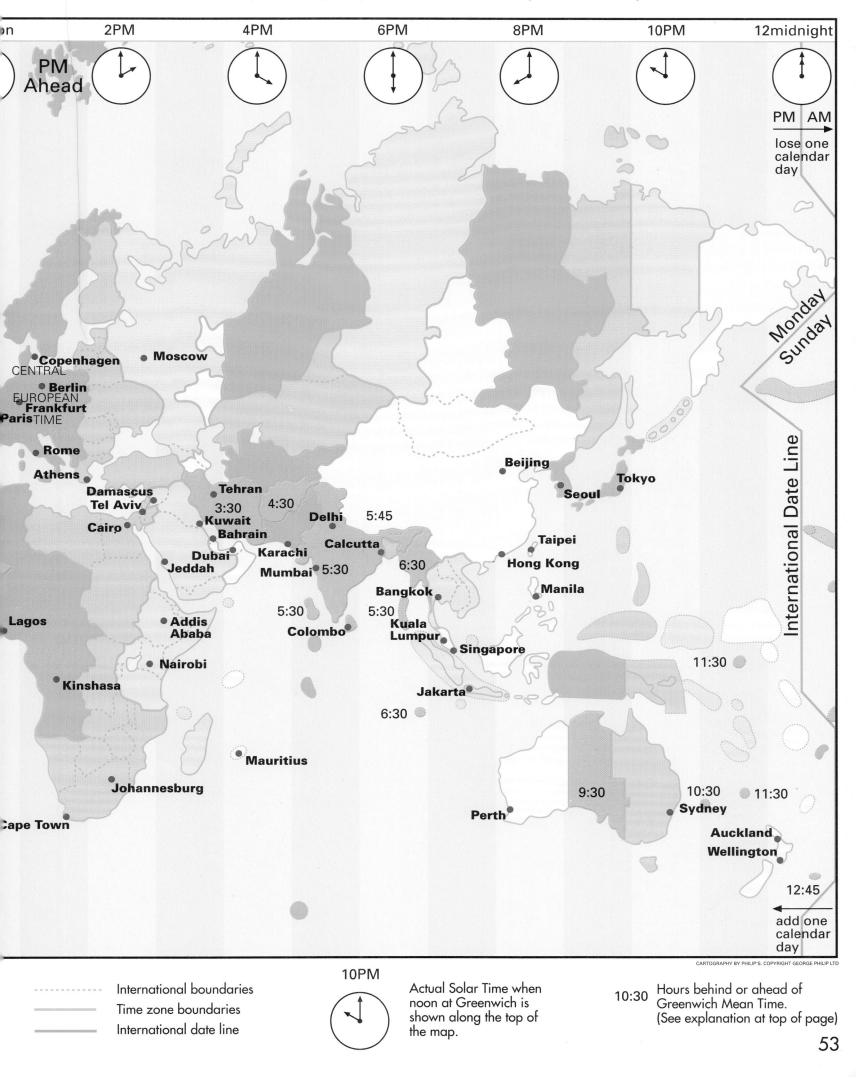

CARTOGRAPHY BY PHILIP'S. COPYRIGHT GEORGE PHILIP LTD

World's Highest Peaks			
①	Himalayas:	Mt. Everest	8848m
②	Hindu Kush:	K2	8611m
③	Andes:	Aconcagua	6960m
④	Rocky Mts:	Mt. McKinley	6194m
⑤	East Africa:	Kilimanjaro	5895m
⑥	Caucasus:	Elbrus	5633m
⑦	Antarctica:	Vinson Massif	5139m
⑧	Alps:	Mt. Blanc	4807m

Mountains – Bonney Range in British Columbia, Canada

Hills – Burgundy, France
2 *Hills – Burgundy, France.*

World's Highest Cities	
⑨	Bogotá, Colombia	2639m
⑩	Addis Ababa, Ethiopia	2362m
⑪	Mexico City, Mexico	2240m
⑫	Nairobi, Kenya	1820m
⑬	Johannesburg, South Africa	1734m
⑭	Denver, U.S.A.	1609m
⑮	Salt Lake City, U.S.A.	1310m
⑯	Calgary, Canada	1049m
⑰	São Paulo, Brazil	776m
⑱	Ankara, Turkey	686m

Place Equator on this line

World's Largest Deserts		
⑲	Sahara, North Africa	9 000 000 km²
⑳	Australian, Australia	3 830 000 km²
㉑	Arabian, Southwest Asia	1 300 000 km²
㉒	Gobi, Central Asia	1 295 000 km²
㉓	Kalahari, Southern Africa	520 000 km²
㉔	Turkestan, Central Asia	450 000 km²
㉕	Takla Makan, China	327 000 km²
㉖	Sonoran, U.S.A./Mexico	310 000 km²
㉗	Namib, Southwest Africa	310 000 km²
㉘	Thar, Northwest India/ Pakistan	260 000 km²

Mountains
Hills
Plateaus
Plains
Land under ice
Seas and Lakes

eau – Grand Canyon, Arizona, U.S.A.

Plains – Northern Territory, Australia.

Land under ice – Antarctic Peninsula

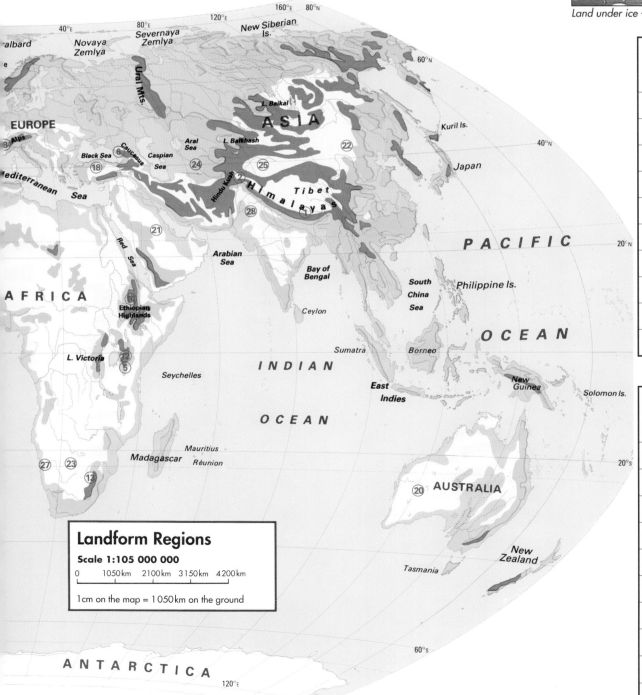

Landform Regions

Scale 1:105 000 000

0   1050km   2100km   3150km   4200km

1cm on the map = 1050km on the ground

Countries with largest water areas	
Canada	754 093 km²
India	314 399 km²
China	270 550 km²
U.S.A.	206 010 km²
Ethiopia	120 900 km²
Colombia	100 209 km²
Indonesia	92 999 km²
Russia	79 400 km²
Australia	68 920 km²
Tanzania	59 049 km²

Countries with longest coastlines	
Canada	90 908 km
Indonesia	54 716 km
Greenland	44 087 km
Russia	37 650 km
Australia	25 760 km
Philippines	22 540 km
United States	19 924 km
Norway	16 093 km
New Zealand	15 134 km
China	14 500 km

Climates of the World

Tropical climate (hot and wet)	Dry climate (desert and steppe)	Mild climate (warm and wet)	Continental climate (cold and wet)	Polar climate (very cold and dry)	Mountainous areas (where altitude affects climate type)

Heavy rainfall and high temperatures all the year with little difference in temperature throughout the year.

Many months, often years, without rain. High temperatures in the summer but cooler in winter.

Rain every month. Warm summers and cool winters.

Mild summers and very cold winters.

Very cold at all times, especially in the winter months. Very little rainfall.

Lower temperatures because the land is high. Heavy rain and snow.

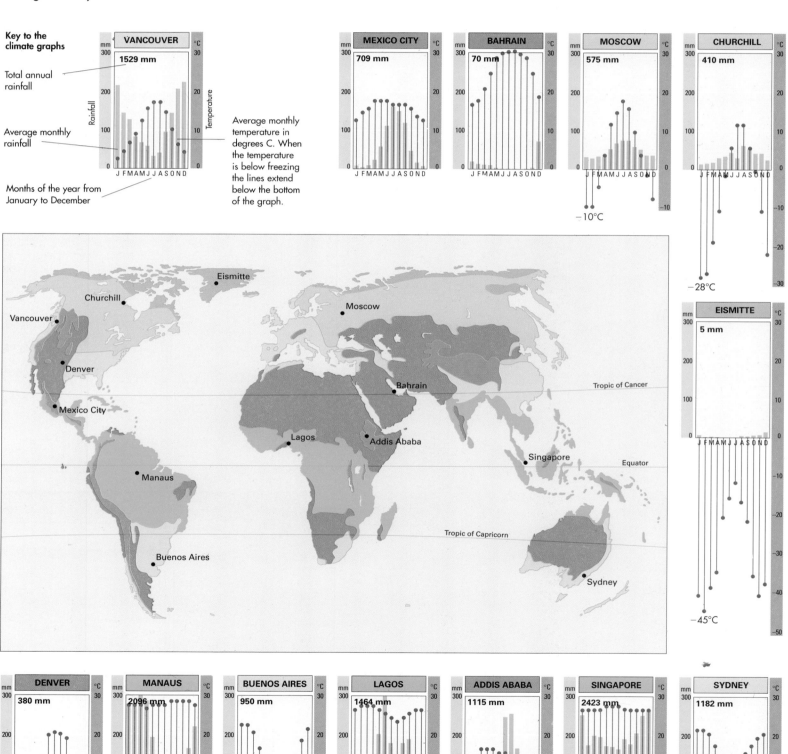

Key to the climate graphs

Total annual rainfall

Average monthly rainfall

Months of the year from January to December

Average monthly temperature in degrees C. When the temperature is below freezing the lines extend below the bottom of the graph.

VANCOUVER — 1529 mm
MEXICO CITY — 709 mm
BAHRAIN — 70 mm
MOSCOW — 575 mm — −10°C
CHURCHILL — 410 mm — −28°C
EISMITTE — 5 mm — −45°C
DENVER — 380 mm
MANAUS — 2096 mm
BUENOS AIRES — 950 mm
LAGOS — 1464 mm
ADDIS ABABA — 1115 mm
SINGAPORE — 2423 mm
SYDNEY — 1182 mm

Tropic of Cancer
Equator
Tropic of Capricorn

56

CARTOGRAPHY BY PHILIP'S. COPYRIGHT GEORGE PHILIP LTD

Annual rainfall

Human, plant and animal life cannot live without water. The map on the right shows how much rain falls in different parts of the world. You can see that there is a lot of rain in some places near the Equator. In other places, like the desert areas of the world, there is very little rain. Few plants or animals can survive there. There is also very little precipitation in the polar regions of the north because the air is too cold to hold much moisture.

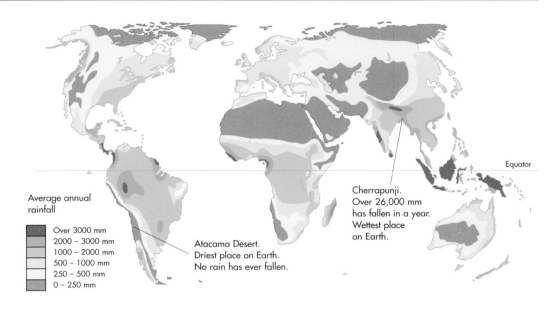

Average annual rainfall

Over 3000 mm
2000 – 3000 mm
1000 – 2000 mm
500 – 1000 mm
250 – 500 mm
0 – 250 mm

Atacama Desert. Driest place on Earth. No rain has ever fallen.

Cherrapunji. Over 26,000 mm has fallen in a year. Wettest place on Earth.

Equator

January temperature

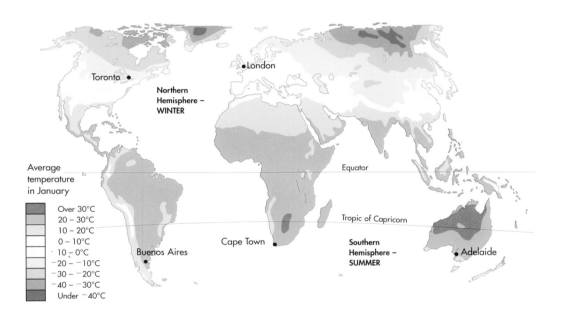

Toronto

London

Northern Hemisphere – WINTER

Average temperature in January

Over 30°C
20 – 30°C
10 – 20°C
0 – 10°C
−10 – 0°C
−20 – −10°C
−30 – −20°C
−40 – −30°C
Under −40°C

Equator

Buenos Aires

Cape Town

Tropic of Capricorn

Southern Hemisphere – SUMMER

Adelaide

In December, it is winter in the northern hemisphere. It is hot in the southern continents and cold in the northern continents. The North Pole is tilted away from the sun. The sun is overhead in the regions around the Tropic of Capricorn to give longer days in the southern hemisphere. This means that there are about 14 hours of daylight in Buenos Aires, Cape Town and Adelaide, and only about 8 hours in London and Toronto.

June temperature

In June, it is summer in the northern hemisphere and winter in the southern hemisphere. It is warmer in the northern continents and colder in the southern continents. The North Pole is tilted towards the sun. It is overhead in regions around the Tropic of Cancer to give longer days in the northern hemisphere. In London and Toronto there are about 16 hours of daylight, but in Buenos Aires, Cape Town and Adelaide there are just under 10 hours.

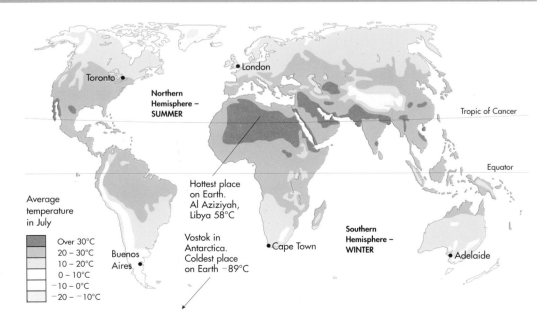

Toronto

London

Northern Hemisphere – SUMMER

Tropic of Cancer

Average temperature in July

Over 30°C
20 – 30°C
10 – 20°C
0 – 10°C
−10 – 0°C
−20 – −10°C

Buenos Aires

Hottest place on Earth. Al Aziziyah, Libya 58°C

Vostok in Antarctica. Coldest place on Earth −89°C

Cape Town

Southern Hemisphere – WINTER

Equator

Adelaide

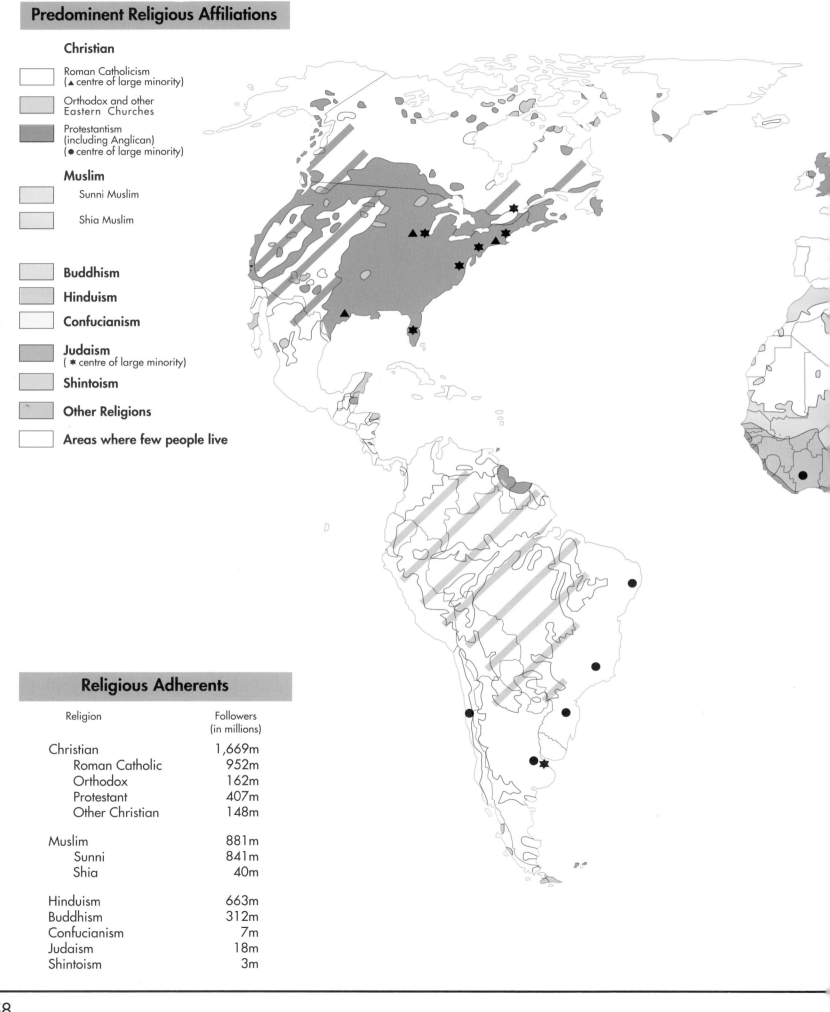

Predominent Religious Affiliations

Christian

Roman Catholicism
(▲ centre of large minority)

Orthodox and other
Eastern Churches

Protestantism
(including Anglican)
(● centre of large minority)

Muslim

Sunni Muslim

Shia Muslim

Buddhism

Hinduism

Confucianism

Judaism
(✴ centre of large minority)

Shintoism

Other Religions

Areas where few people live

Religious Adherents

Religion	Followers (in millions)
Christian	1,669m
Roman Catholic	952m
Orthodox	162m
Protestant	407m
Other Christian	148m
Muslim	881m
Sunni	841m
Shia	40m
Hinduism	663m
Buddhism	312m
Confucianism	7m
Judaism	18m
Shintoism	3m

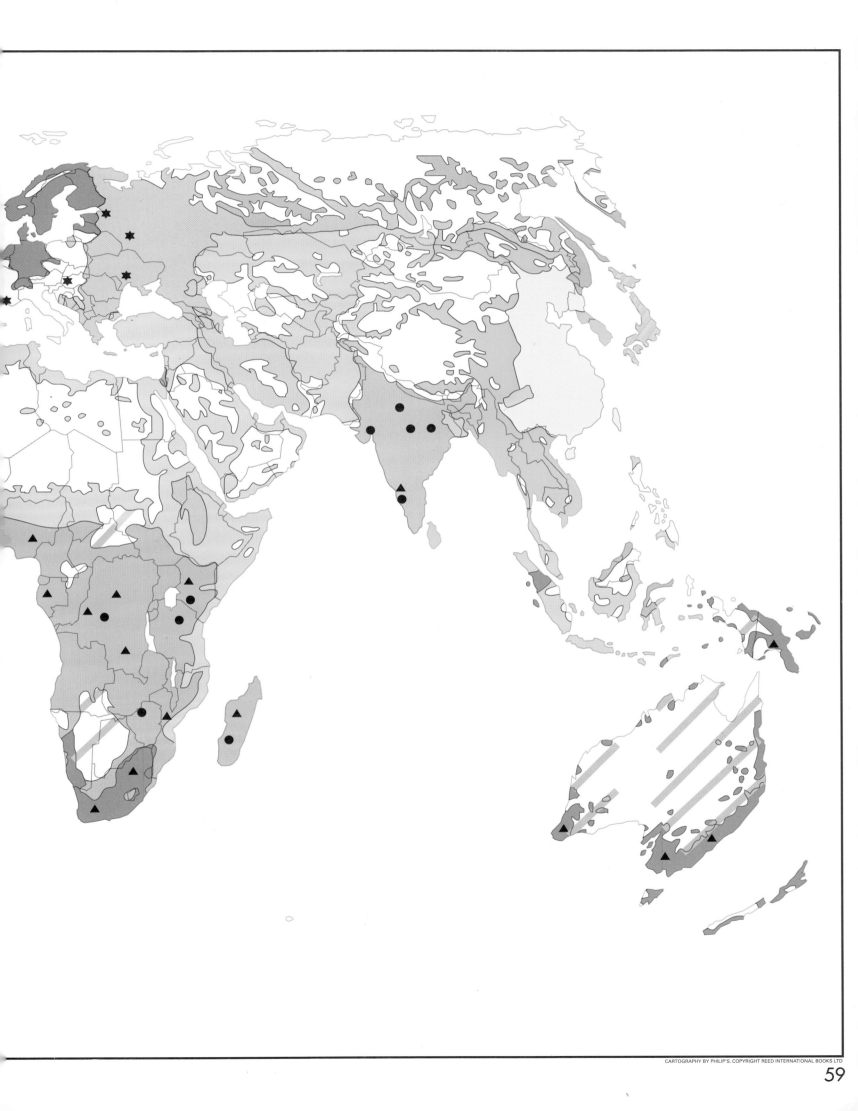

Natural Disasters

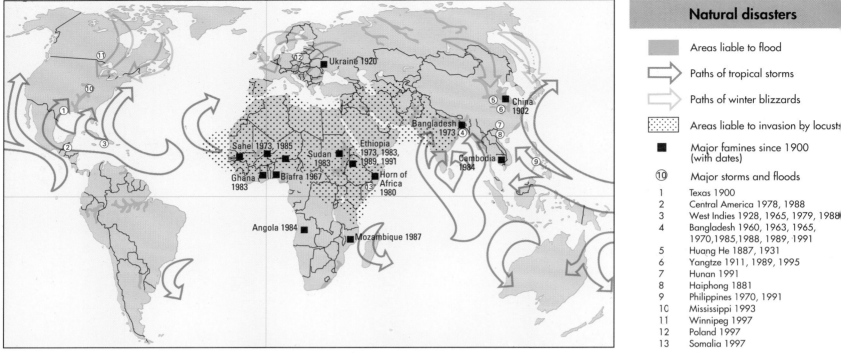

Natural disasters

	Areas liable to flood
⇨	Paths of tropical storms
⇨	Paths of winter blizzards
░	Areas liable to invasion by locusts
■	Major famines since 1900 (with dates)
⑩	Major storms and floods

1 Texas 1900
2 Central America 1978, 1988
3 West Indies 1928, 1965, 1979, 1988
4 Bangladesh 1960, 1963, 1965, 1970, 1985, 1988, 1989, 1991
5 Huang He 1887, 1931
6 Yangtze 1911, 1989, 1995
7 Hunan 1991
8 Haiphong 1881
9 Philippines 1970, 1991
10 Mississippi 1993
11 Winnipeg 1997
12 Poland 1997
13 Somalia 1997

Hurricanes are violent storms that form above the oceans in certain regions near the equator. The winds of a hurricane blow in a circular motion around an area known as an "eye". In the "eye of the storm", the winds stop and the clouds disappear but the ocean is still rough.

Hurricanes develop when warm, moist air is forced upwards by heavier, cooler air. Wind speeds in hurricanes vary from 120 kms/hour to more than 250 kms/hour. Damage to property from wind and water can be great, especially in coastal regions. Hurricane-type storms in the western Pacific are called typhoons.

A **tornado** is a violent whirling wind, usually in the form of a funnel-shaped cloud, that moves along land. Tornadoes are most common in temperate latitudes and can occur when strong updrafts and weather fronts move through an area. Funnel winds have been recorded at more than 480 kms/hour.

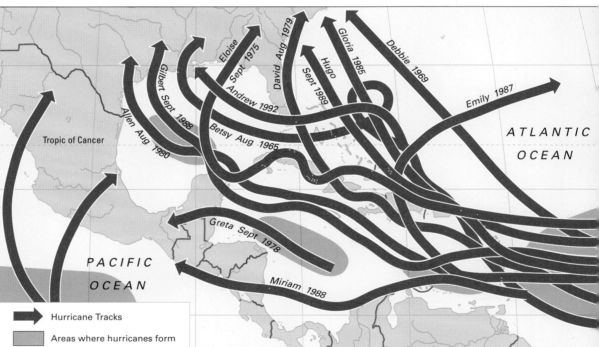

Hurricane Gladys as seen from Apollo 7

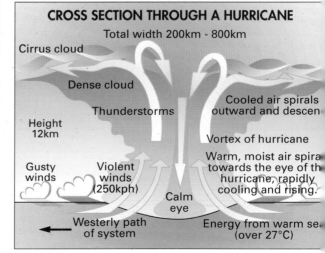

CROSS SECTION THROUGH A HURRICANE

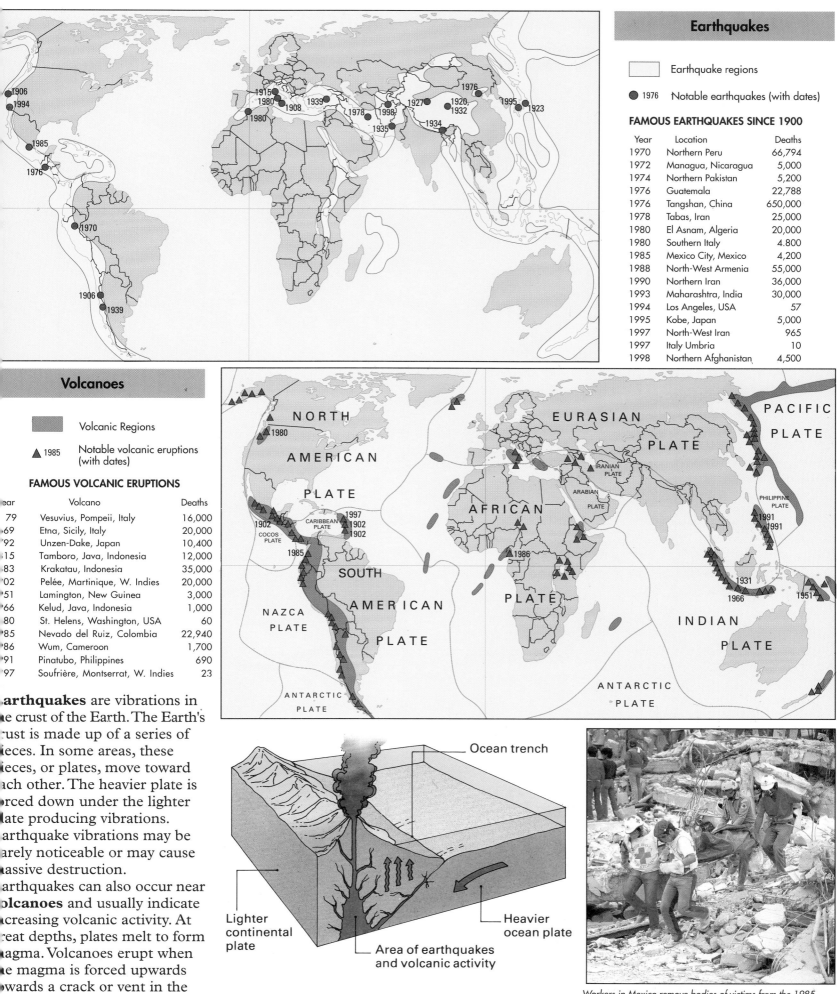

	Earthquake regions
● 1976	Notable earthquakes (with dates)

FAMOUS EARTHQUAKES SINCE 1900

Year	Location	Deaths
1970	Northern Peru	66,794
1972	Managua, Nicaragua	5,000
1974	Northern Pakistan	5,200
1976	Guatemala	22,788
1976	Tangshan, China	650,000
1978	Tabas, Iran	25,000
1980	El Asnam, Algeria	20,000
1980	Southern Italy	4.800
1985	Mexico City, Mexico	4,200
1988	North-West Armenia	55,000
1990	Northern Iran	36,000
1993	Maharashtra, India	30,000
1994	Los Angeles, USA	57
1995	Kobe, Japan	5,000
1997	North-West Iran	965
1997	Italy Umbria	10
1998	Northern Afghanistan	4,500

Volcanoes

	Volcanic Regions
▲ 1985	Notable volcanic eruptions (with dates)

FAMOUS VOLCANIC ERUPTIONS

Year	Volcano	Deaths
79	Vesuvius, Pompeii, Italy	16,000
1669	Etna, Sicily, Italy	20,000
1792	Unzen-Dake, Japan	10,400
1815	Tamboro, Java, Indonesia	12,000
1883	Krakatau, Indonesia	35,000
1902	Pelée, Martinique, W. Indies	20,000
1951	Lamington, New Guinea	3,000
1966	Kelud, Java, Indonesia	1,000
1980	St. Helens, Washington, USA	60
1985	Nevado del Ruiz, Colombia	22,940
1986	Wum, Cameroon	1,700
1991	Pinatubo, Philippines	690
1997	Soufrière, Montserrat, W. Indies	23

Earthquakes are vibrations in the crust of the Earth. The Earth's crust is made up of a series of pieces. In some areas, these pieces, or plates, move toward each other. The heavier plate is forced down under the lighter plate producing vibrations. Earthquake vibrations may be barely noticeable or may cause massive destruction. Earthquakes can also occur near **volcanoes** and usually indicate increasing volcanic activity. At great depths, plates melt to form magma. Volcanoes erupt when the magma is forced upwards towards a crack or vent in the Earth's crust.

Ocean trench

Lighter continental plate

Area of earthquakes and volcanic activity

Heavier ocean plate

Workers in Mexico remove bodies of victims from the 1985 earthquake that killed thousands of people.

— Peoples and Cities of the World —

Where people live (population distribution)

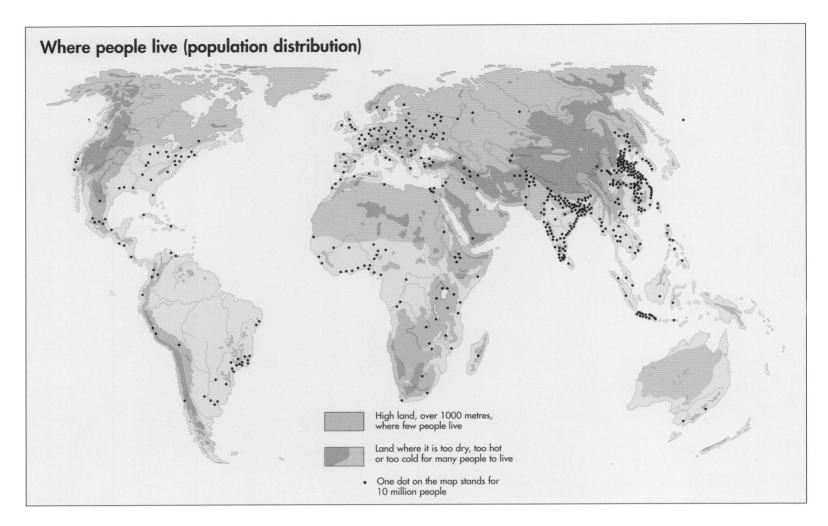

High land, over 1000 metres, where few people live

Land where it is too dry, too hot or too cold for many people to live

· One dot on the map stands for 10 million people

The growth of the population of the world 1000 – 2000 AD

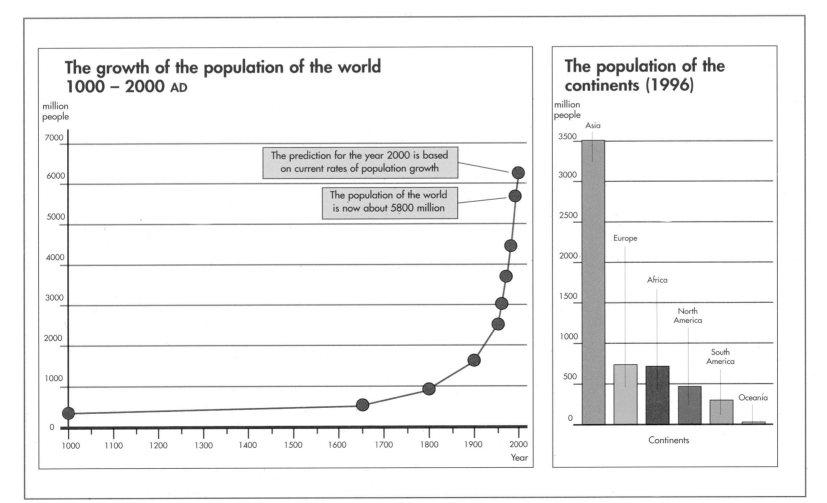

million people

The prediction for the year 2000 is based on current rates of population growth

The population of the world is now about 5800 million

Year

The population of the continents (1996)

million people

Asia

Europe

Africa

North America

South America

Oceania

Continents

The world's largest cities (1996)

(population in millions)

Tokyo	27
Sao Paulo	16
New York	16
Mexico City	16
Bombay (Mumbai)	15
Shanghai	15
Los Angeles	12
Beijing	12
Calcutta (Kolkata)	12
Seoul	12
Jakarta	12
Buenos Aires	11
Tianjin	11
Osaka	11
Lagos	10
Rio de Janeiro	10
Delhi	10
Karachi	10
Cairo	10
Paris	9
Manila	9
Moscow	9
Chicago	8
Dhaka	8
Istanbul	7
London	7

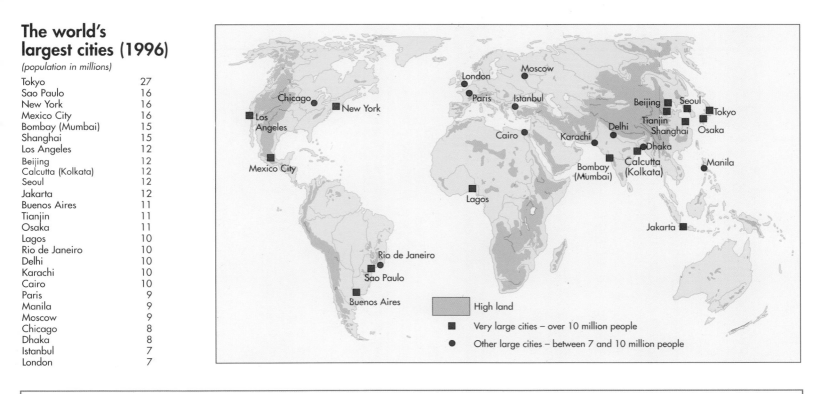

High land

■ Very large cities – over 10 million people

● Other large cities – between 7 and 10 million people

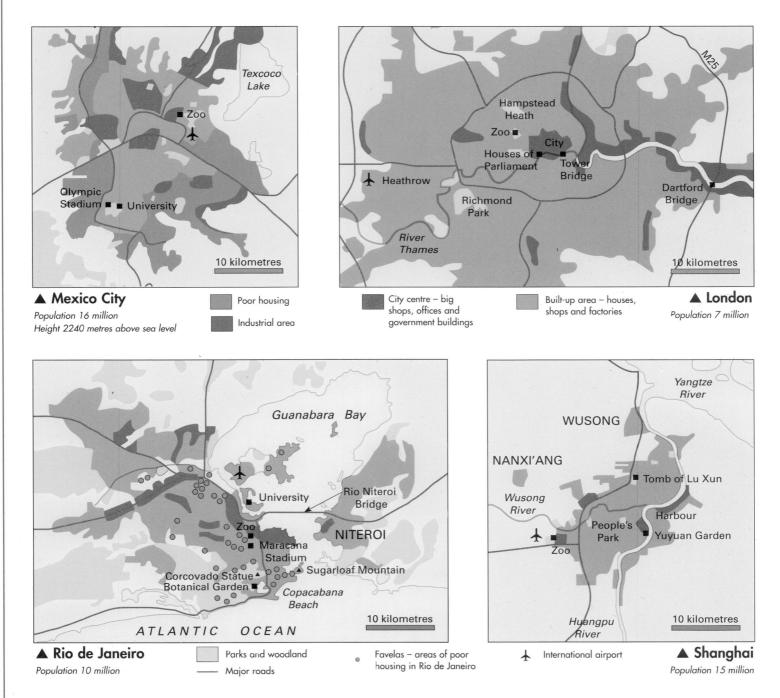

▲ **Mexico City**

Population 16 million
Height 2240 metres above sea level

Poor housing

Industrial area

City centre – big shops, offices and government buildings

Built-up area – houses, shops and factories

▲ **London**

Population 7 million

▲ **Rio de Janeiro**

Population 10 million

Parks and woodland

— Major roads

● Favelas – areas of poor housing in Rio de Janeiro

✈ International airport

▲ **Shanghai**

Population 15 million

Rivers

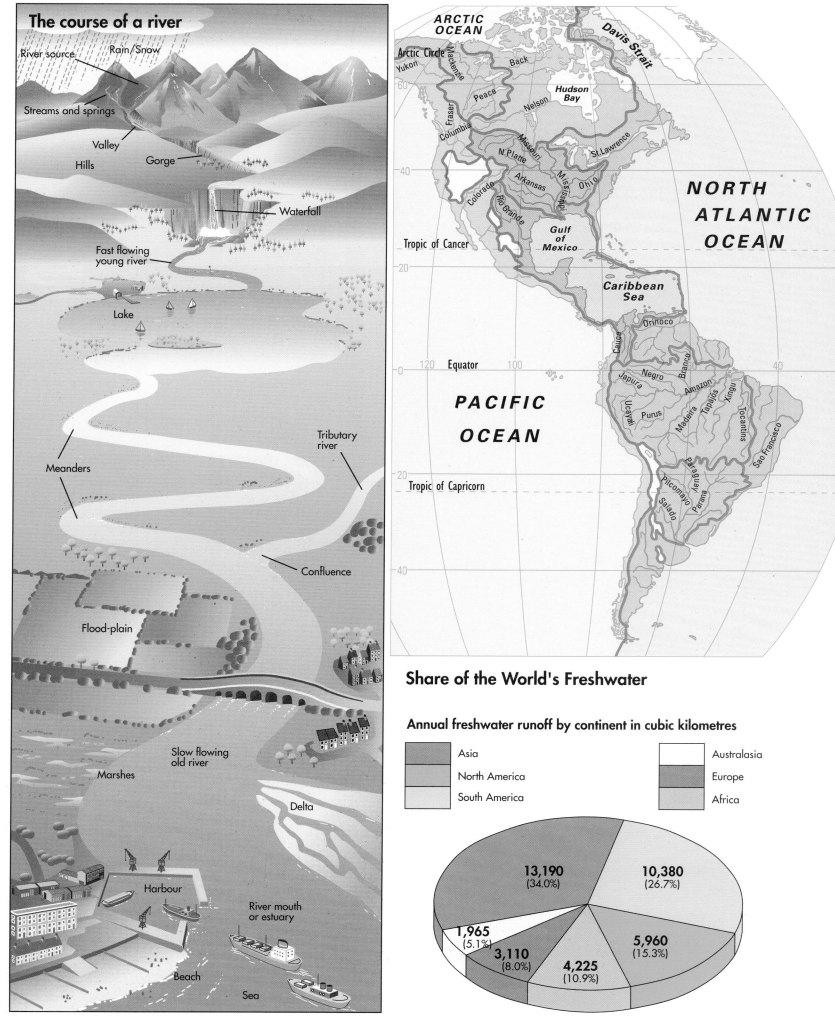

The course of a river

- River source
- Rain/Snow
- Streams and springs
- Valley
- Hills
- Gorge
- Waterfall
- Fast flowing young river
- Lake
- Meanders
- Tributary river
- Confluence
- Flood-plain
- Slow flowing old river
- Marshes
- Delta
- Harbour
- River mouth or estuary
- Beach
- Sea

ARCTIC OCEAN
Davis Strait
Arctic Circle
Yukon
Mackenzie
Back
Peace
Nelson
Hudson Bay
Fraser
Columbia
Missouri
St.Lawrence
N.Platte
Arkansas
Mississippi
Ohio
Colorado
Rio Grande
Gulf of Mexico

NORTH ATLANTIC OCEAN

Tropic of Cancer

Caribbean Sea

Orinoco
Cauca
Negro
Branco
Japura
Amazon
Xingu
Ucayali
Purus
Madeira
Tapajós
Tocantins
Sao Francisco
Paraguay
Pilcomayo
Parana
Salado

PACIFIC OCEAN

Equator
120   100   80   40

Tropic of Capricorn

40   60   40   20   0   20   40

Share of the World's Freshwater

Annual freshwater runoff by continent in cubic kilometres

- Asia
- North America
- South America
- Australasia
- Europe
- Africa

- 13,190 (34.0%)
- 10,380 (26.7%)
- 1,965 (5.1%)
- 3,110 (8.0%)
- 4,225 (10.9%)
- 5,960 (15.3%)

64

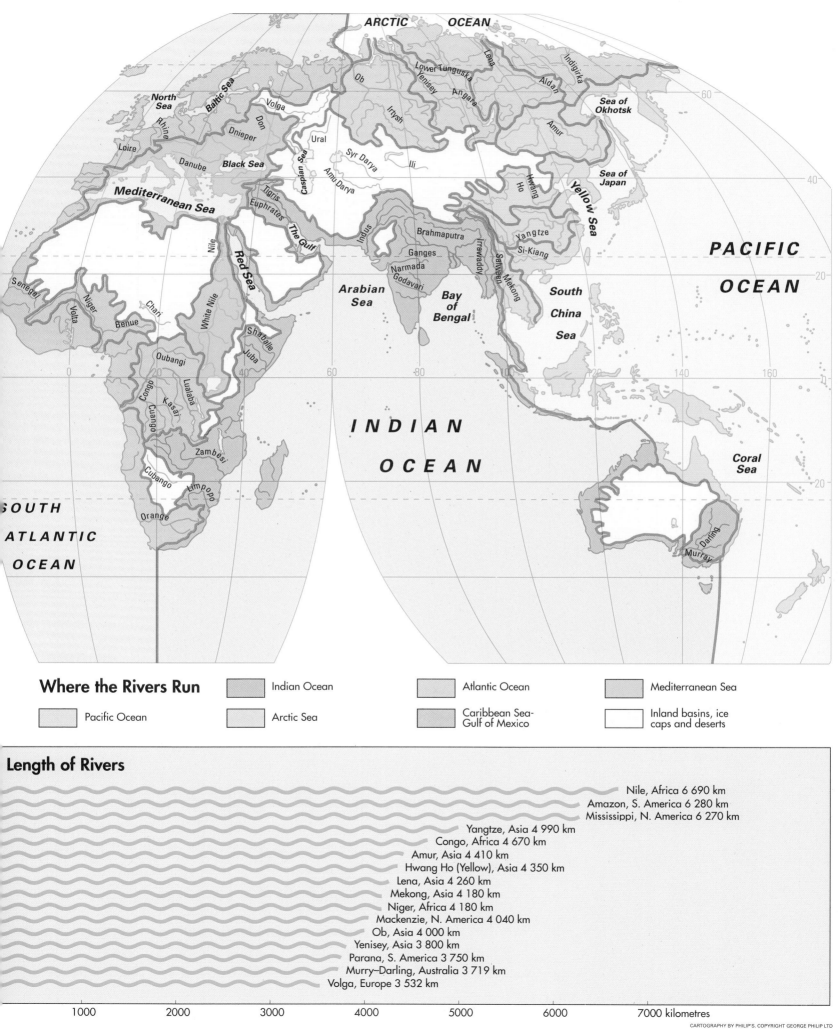

Where the Rivers Run

- Indian Ocean
- Atlantic Ocean
- Mediterranean Sea
- Pacific Ocean
- Arctic Sea
- Caribbean Sea-Gulf of Mexico
- Inland basins, ice caps and deserts

Length of Rivers

Nile, Africa 6 690 km
Amazon, S. America 6 280 km
Mississippi, N. America 6 270 km
Yangtze, Asia 4 990 km
Congo, Africa 4 670 km
Amur, Asia 4 410 km
Hwang Ho (Yellow), Asia 4 350 km
Lena, Asia 4 260 km
Mekong, Asia 4 180 km
Niger, Africa 4 180 km
Mackenzie, N. America 4 040 km
Ob, Asia 4 000 km
Yenisey, Asia 3 800 km
Parana, S. America 3 750 km
Murry–Darling, Australia 3 719 km
Volga, Europe 3 532 km

| 1000 | 2000 | 3000 | 4000 | 5000 | 6000 | 7000 kilometres |

World Vegetation

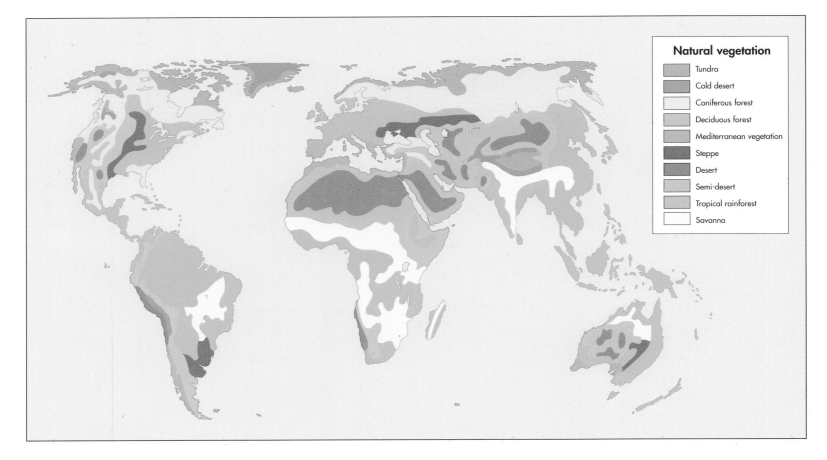

Natural vegetation
- Tundra
- Cold desert
- Coniferous forest
- Deciduous forest
- Mediterranean vegetation
- Steppe
- Desert
- Semi-desert
- Tropical rainforest
- Savanna

The map above shows the location of the types of vegetation found around the world. The vegetation belts reflect the influence of climate.

The diagram below shows the types of plants which grow on mountains.

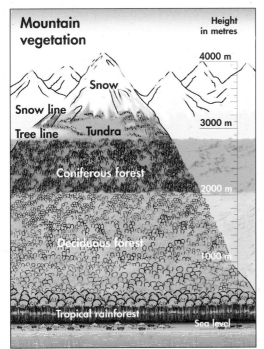

Tundra
Long, dry, very cold winters. Grasses, moss, bog and dwarf trees.

Cold desert
Very cold with little rain or snow. Few plants can thrive.

Coniferous forest
Harsh winters, mild summers. Trees have leaves all year.

Deciduous forest
Rain all year, cool winters. Trees shed leaves in winter.

Mediterranean
Hot, dry summers. Mild wet winters. Plants adapt to the heat and dryness.

Steppe
Some rain with a dry season. Grasslands with scattered trees.

Desert
Little rainfall. Plants only grow continuously at oases with underground water. Other plants spring to life when rain does fall.

Semi-desert
Low rainfall, sparse vegetation. Grass with scattered trees, particularly along stream beds.

Tropical rainforest (jungle)
Very hot and wet all the year. Tall trees and lush vegetation support a wide variety of animal life.

Savanna
Mainly dry, but lush grass grows when the rains come. Trees are scattered across the landscape and increase in number closer to the rainforest.

Tundra

Pingo (mound)

Thin, stony soil with permafrost below

Mosses, lichens and herbs

Cold desert

No plants can grow

Coniferous forest

Evergreen conifers (spruces and firs)

Young tree saplings and small shrubs

Carpet of pine needles

Ferns and brambles on edge of forest

Yearly cycle of a deciduous forest

Spring

Summer

Autumn

Winter

Mediterranean

Small stunted trees

Scrub

Steppe *There are many plants in the steppe grasslands.*

People planting crops damages the natural habitat.

Tropical rainforest

Scattered trees with umbrella-shaped tops grow the highest.

Main layer of tall trees growing close together.

Creepers grow up the trees to reach the sunlight.

Ferns, mosses and small plants grow closest to the ground.

Desert

Sand blown into dunes by the wind

Palm trees

Cactus

Oasis

Semi-desert

Joshua trees

Grass and bush

Savanna Dry season

Wet season

—Agriculture, Forests and Fishing—

How the land is used

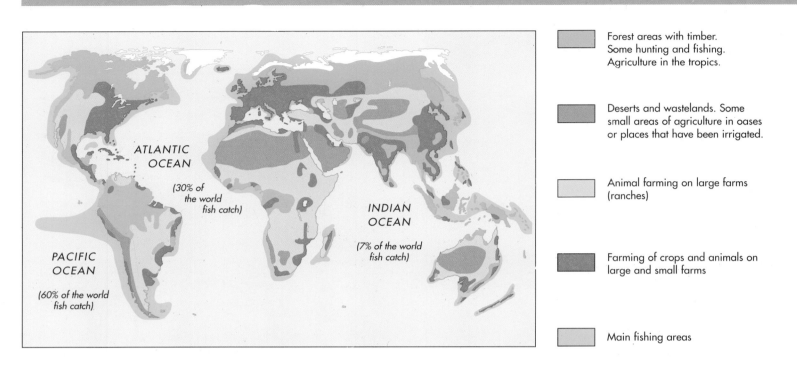

Forest areas with timber. Some hunting and fishing. Agriculture in the tropics.

Deserts and wastelands. Some small areas of agriculture in oases or places that have been irrigated.

Animal farming on large farms (ranches)

Farming of crops and animals on large and small farms

Main fishing areas

The importance of agriculture

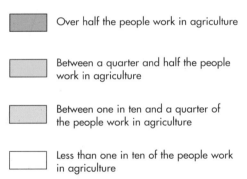

Over half the people work in agriculture

Between a quarter and half the people work in agriculture

Between one in ten and a quarter of the people work in agriculture

Less than one in ten of the people work in agriculture

Countries which depend on agriculture for over half their income

A hundred years ago about 80% of the world's population worked in agriculture. Today it is only about 40% but agriculture is still very important in some countries.

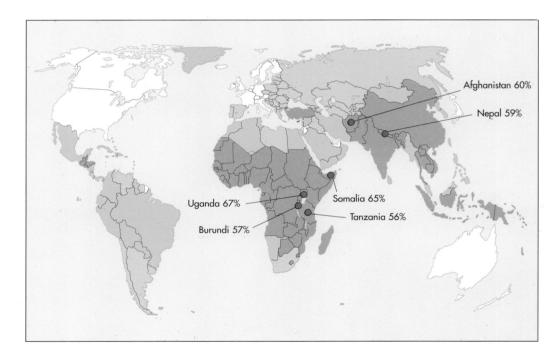

Afghanistan 60%

Nepal 59%

Uganda 67%

Somalia 65%

Burundi 57%

Tanzania 56%

Methods of fishing

There are two types of sea fishing:

1. **Deep-sea fishing** using large trawlers which often stay at sea for many weeks.

2. **Inshore fishing** using small boats, traps and nets up to 70 km from the coast.

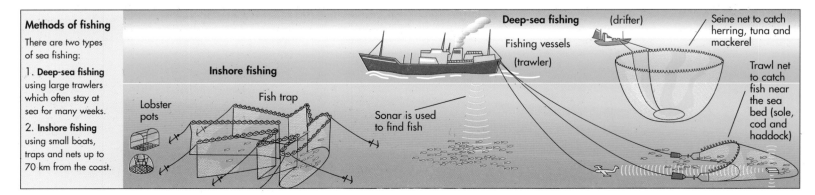

Inshore fishing

Lobster pots

Fish trap

Sonar is used to find fish

Deep-sea fishing   (drifter)

Fishing vessels (trawler)

Seine net to catch herring, tuna and mackerel

Trawl net to catch fish near the sea bed (sole, cod and haddock)

Wheat and rice

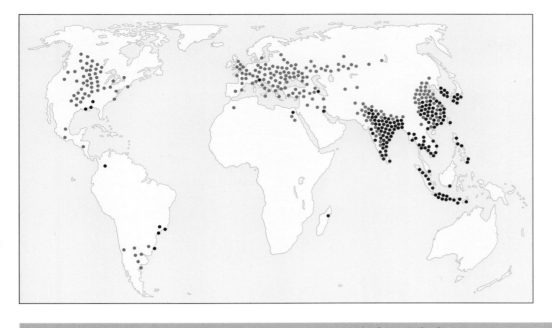

- One dot stands for 2 million tonnes of wheat produced
- One dot stands for 2 million tonnes of rice produced

Wheat is the main cereal crop grown in cooler regions. Rice is the main food for over half the people in the world. It is grown in water in paddy fields in tropical areas. Over a third of the world's rice is grown in China.

Cattle and sheep

- One dot stands for 10 million cattle
- One dot stands for 10 million sheep

Meat, milk and leather come from cattle. The map shows that they are kept in most parts of the world except where it is hot or very cold. Sheep are kept in cooler regions and they can live on poorer grassland than cows. Sheep are reared for meat and wool.

Timber

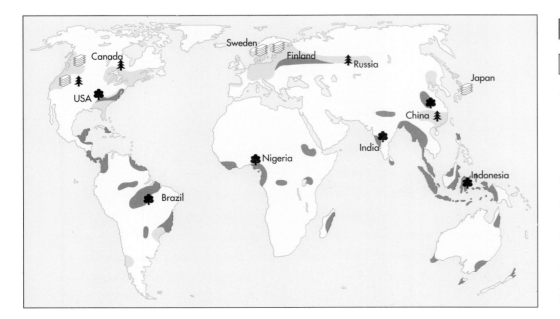

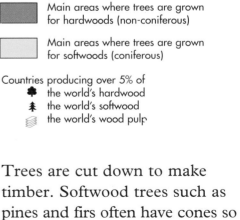

- Main areas where trees are grown for hardwoods (non-coniferous)
- Main areas where trees are grown for softwoods (coniferous)

Countries producing over 5% of
- the world's hardwood
- the world's softwood
- the world's wood pulp

Trees are cut down to make timber. Softwood trees such as pines and firs often have cones so they are called coniferous. Some trees are chopped up into wood pulp which is used to make paper.

Minerals and Energy

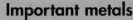

Important metals

 Iron ore
▲ Bauxite
● Copper

Iron is the most important metal in manufacturing. It is mixed with other metals to make steel which is used for ships, cars and machinery. Bauxite ore is used to make aluminum. Because aluminum is light and strong, it is used to make aeroplanes. Copper is a good conductor, so it is used for electric wires and cooking utensils. It is also used in making brass and bronze.

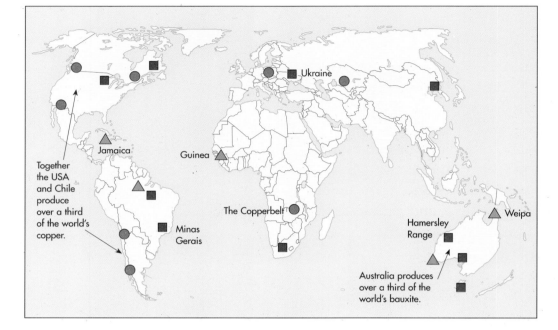

Precious metals and minerals

⬮ Gold
☆ Silver
◆ Diamonds

Some minerals like gold, silver and diamonds are used to make jewellery. They are also important in industry. Diamonds are the hardest mineral and so they are used to make tools that cut or grind. Silver is used in photography to coat film, and to make electrical goods. Both gold and silver are used in the electronics industry and to make jewellery.

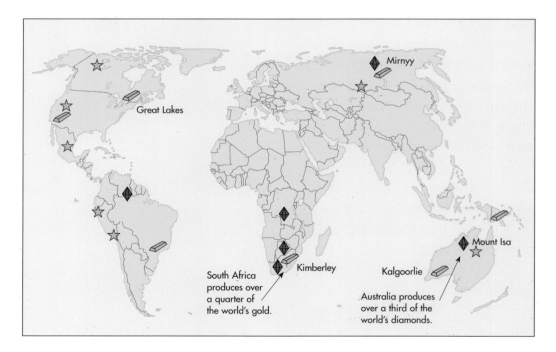

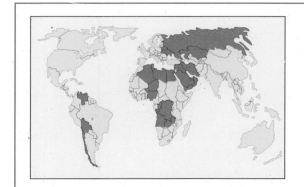

There are over 70 different types of metals and minerals in the world. The maps above show the main countries where some of the most important metals and minerals are mined. After mining, metals and fuels are often exported to other countries where they are manufactured into goods. The map on the left shows which countries depend most on mining for their exports and wealth. These countries are coloured red.

Oil and gas

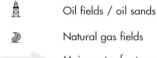

Oil fields / oil sands

Natural gas fields

Main routes for transporting oil and gas by tanker

Crude oil is drilled from deep in the Earth's crust. The oil is then refined so that it can be used in different industries. Oil is used to make gasoline and is also very important in the chemical industry. Natural gas is often found in the same places as oil, and is used for heating and cooking.

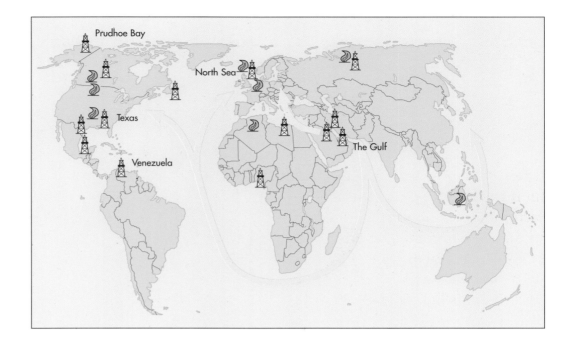

Coal

Lignite (soft brown coal)

Hard coal (bituminous)

Main routes for transporting coal.

Coal is a fuel that comes from forests and swamps that rotted millions of years ago and have been crushed by layers of rock. The coal is cut out of the rock from deep mines and also from open-pit mines where the coal is nearer the surface. The oldest type of coal is hard and is most often used to create energy for factories. The coal formed more recently is softer.

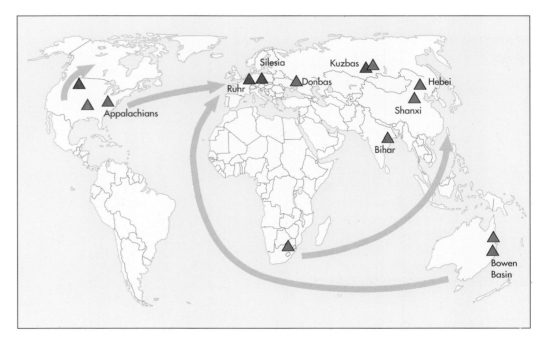

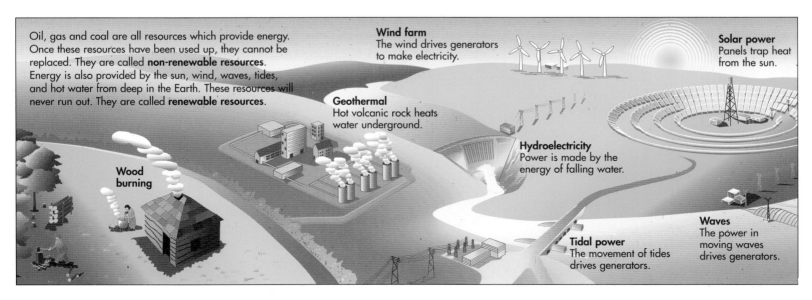

Oil, gas and coal are all resources which provide energy. Once these resources have been used up, they cannot be replaced. They are called **non-renewable resources**. Energy is also provided by the sun, wind, waves, tides, and hot water from deep in the Earth. These resources will never run out. They are called **renewable resources**.

Wind farm
The wind drives generators to make electricity.

Solar power
Panels trap heat from the sun.

Geothermal
Hot volcanic rock heats water underground.

Hydroelectricity
Power is made by the energy of falling water.

Wood burning

Tidal power
The movement of tides drives generators.

Waves
The power in moving waves drives generators.

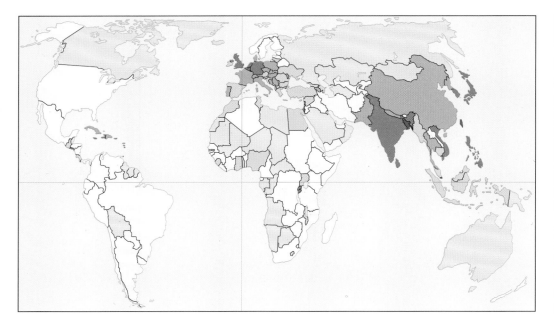

Population density by country

Density of people per square kilometre 1997

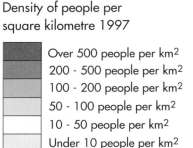

- Over 500 people per km²
- 200 - 500 people per km²
- 100 - 200 people per km²
- 50 - 100 people per km²
- 10 - 50 people per km²
- Under 10 people per km²

Exampl
China
111 peop

Canad
3 people

A country's population density is obtaine by dividing its total population by its to area. A population density map gives an id of how crowded a country is, but does n show where the crowded areas are within t country.

Population change 1990 – 2000

The predicted population change for the years 1990-2000

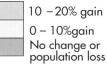

- Over 40% gain
- 30 – 40% gain
- 20 – 30% gain
- 10 – 20% gain
- 0 – 10% gain
- No change or population loss

Populations do not remain the same - they grow as births exceed deaths. Not all countries experience the same rate of growth in population. Countries of the "South" tend to have greater increases in population than countries in the "North" as their birth rates increase or remain steady and their death rates fall.

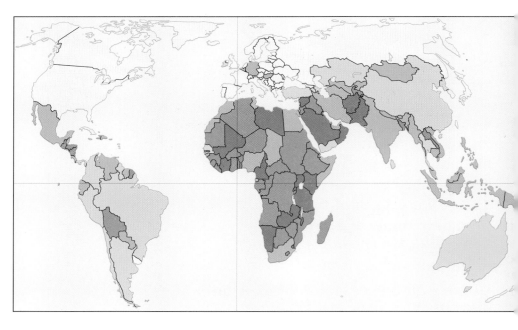

Urban population

Percentage of total population living in towns and cities 1992

- Over 75%
- 50 – 75%
- 25 – 50%
- 10 – 25%
- Under 10%

Up to the 1950's, less than one out of thr people lived in towns and cities. Today it nearly 2 out 3 people. Note how the mair industrial countries have more people livi in towns and cities than those countries th are primarily agricultural.

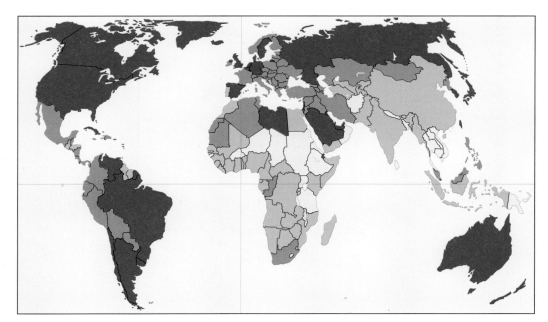

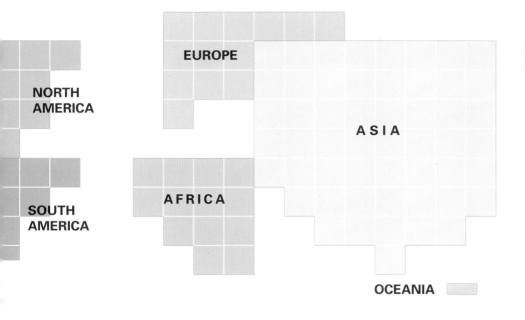

Population by continents

In this diagram the size of each continent is in proportion to its population. Each square represents 1% of the projected world population of 6 122 000 000 in 2000.

Top 10 countries (thousands)

China	1 226 944
India	942 989
U.S.A.	263 563
Indonesia	198 644
Brazil	161 416
Russia	148 385
Pakistan	143 595
Japan	125 156
Bangladesh	118 342
Mexico	93 342

Housing

Number of people per household
(latest available year)

- Over 6 people
- 5 - 6 people
- 4 - 5 people
- 3 - 4 people
- 2 - 3 people
- Under 2 people

In countries with high population growth rates family size tends to be large. This map shows that families in countries in the "South" are larger than in the "North". In developing countries, aunts, uncles and grandparents tend to live with their children creating an extended family.

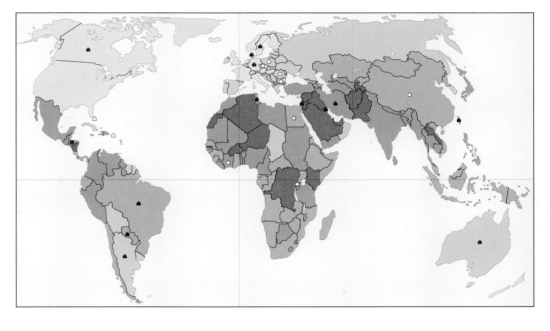

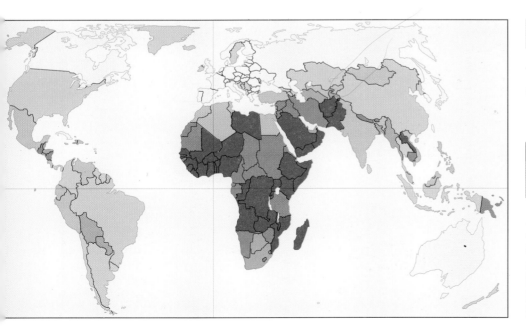

Number of children born

The average number of children a woman can expect to bear during her lifetime 1992

- 6 children or more
- 5 children or more
- 4 children or more
- 3 children or more
- 2 children or more
- 1 child

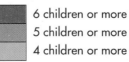

Many factors influence how many children a woman will have : education, work opportunities, availability of birth control information, influences of religion and family income for example. Lowest birth rate occur in wealthier countries in the "North".

World Transportation

Seaways

Main shipping routes

■ The biggest seaports in the world (over 100 million tonnes of cargo handled a year)

● Other big seaports

▨ Ice and icebergs in the sea all the time, or for some part of the year

— Large ships can travel on these rivers

Sea transport is used for goods that are too bulky or heavy to go by air. The main shipping routes are between North America, Europe and the Far East.

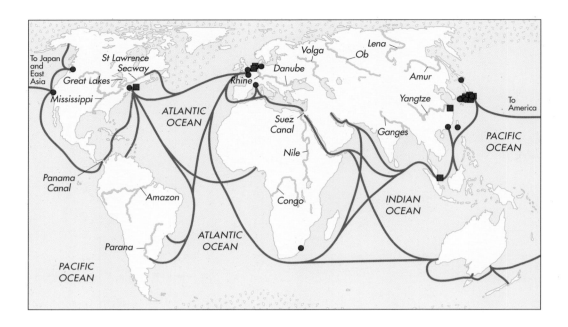

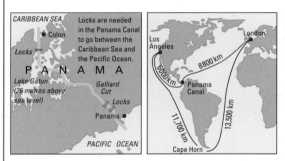

Locks are needed in the Panama Canal to go between the Caribbean Sea and the Pacific Ocean.

CARIBBEAN SEA Colon, Locks, PANAMA, Lake Gatun (26 metres above sea level), Galliard Cut, Locks, Panama, PACIFIC OCEAN

London, Los Angeles, 6000km, 8800 km, 11,700 km, 13,500 km, Panama Canal, Cape Horn

The Panama Canal
Opened in 1914
82 km long
13,000 ships a year

The Suez Canal
Opened in 1870
162 km long
17,000 ships a year

These two important canals cut through narrow pieces of land. Can you work out how much quicker the journeys are by using the canals?

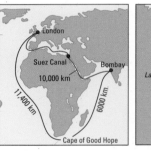

London, Suez Canal, 10,000 km, 11,400 km, 6000 km, Bombay, Cape of Good Hope

Port Said, **MEDITERRANEAN SEA**, The Suez Canal has no locks between the Mediterranean Sea and the Red Sea. **EGYPT**, Lake Timsah, Great Bitter Lake, Little Bitter Lake, Suez, Gulf of Suez

Airways

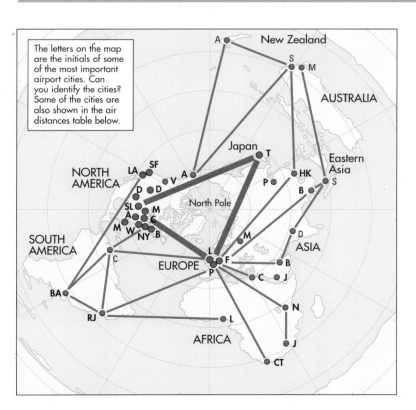

The letters on the map are the initials of some of the most important airport cities. Can you identify the cities? Some of the cities are also shown in the air distances table below.

● Large international airports (over 20 million passengers a year)

● Other important airports

━ Heavily used air routes

— Other important air routes

This map has the North Pole at its centre. It shows how much air traffic connects Europe, North America, Japan and Eastern Asia. You can see the long distances in the USA and Russia that are covered by air.

Air distances (kilometres)

	Buenos Aires	Cape Town	London	Los Angeles	New York	Sydney	Tokyo
Buenos Aires		6880	11,128	9854	8526	11,760	18,338
Cape Town	6880		9672	16,067	12,551	10,982	14,710
London	11,128	9672		8752	5535	17,005	9584
Los Angeles	9854	16,067	8752		3968	12,052	8806
New York	8526	12,551	5535	3968		16,001	10,869
Sydney	11,760	10,982	17,005	12,052	16,001		7809
Tokyo	18,338	14,710	9584	8806	10,869	7809	

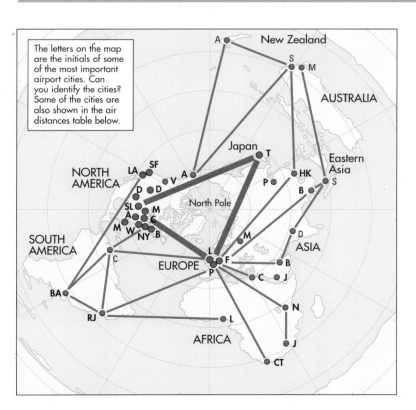

Roads

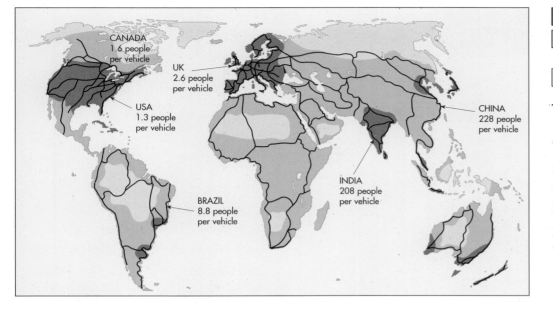

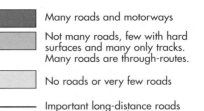

■ Many roads and motorways

Not many roads, few with hard surfaces and many only tracks. Many roads are through-routes.

No roads or very few roads

— Important long-distance roads

This map shows some of the major roads that link important cities and ports. It also shows how many people there are in proportion to the number of vehicles in some countries.

Railways

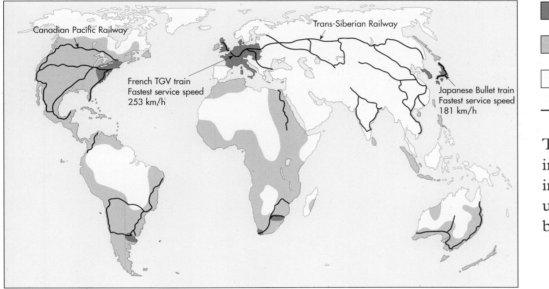

■ Many passenger and goods lines

Scattered railways often taking goods to and from parts of the coast

No rail services or very few rail services

— Important long-distance railways

This map shows some of the important long-distance railways in the world. Railways are often used for transporting goods between cities and to ports.

Pipelines

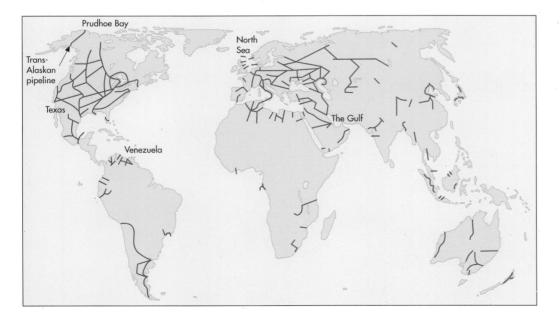

—— Oil and gas pipelines

Pipelines are used for moving oil or gas. Oil and gas are moved to where they will be used or to seaports for loading into tankers to be taken across the sea. The Trans-Alaskan pipeline was built because tankers cannot cross ice. The main oil and gas producing areas of the world are shown on page 39.

Planet in Danger

Expanding deserts

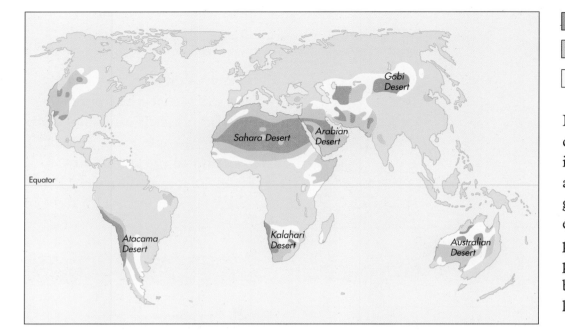

- Existing deserts
- Expanding deserts
- Areas with the risk of becoming desert

In some parts of the world deserts are expanding. This is because trees are cut down and there are too many animals grazing the land near the desert edge. Soils are not managed properly and they become poorer. Gradually farming becomes impossible and the land becomes desert.

Forests in danger

- Tropical forests today
- Tropical forests that have been destroyed or opened up in large areas this century
- Softwood forests that have suffered damage from air pollution, or cutting down too many trees

The tropical forests on Earth are so big that they affect the climate of the whole world. Our tropical forests are getting smaller. They are being cut down for wood and to clear land for ranching, 'slash and burn' farming and mining. These forests play an important role in the production of oxygen.

How does the 'Greenhouse Effect' work?

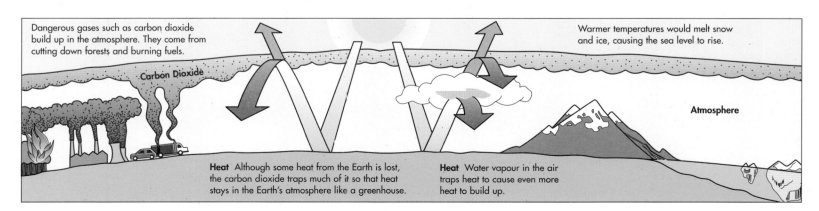

Dangerous gases such as carbon dioxide build up in the atmosphere. They come from cutting down forests and burning fuels.

Warmer temperatures would melt snow and ice, causing the sea level to rise.

Heat Although some heat from the Earth is lost, the carbon dioxide traps much of it so that heat stays in the Earth's atmosphere like a greenhouse.

Heat Water vapour in the air traps heat to cause even more heat to build up.

Pollution

This diagram shows some of the ways that we pollute the land, rivers, sea and air around us. Air pollution causes the Earth's atmosphere to become warmer. This is called the 'Greenhouse Effect' (see the diagram at the bottom of the opposite page). The world's climate is gradually changing because of the 'Greenhouse Effect'.

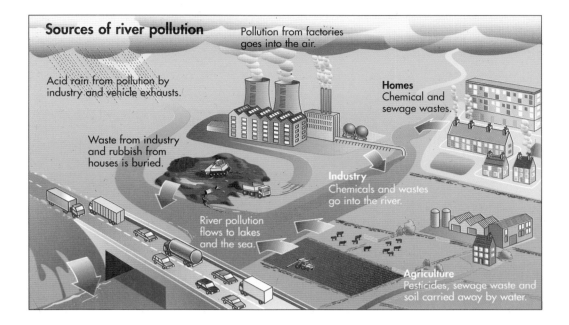

Sources of river pollution

Pollution from factories goes into the air.

Acid rain from pollution by industry and vehicle exhausts.

Waste from industry and rubbish from houses is buried.

River pollution flows to lakes and the sea.

Homes Chemical and sewage wastes.

Industry Chemicals and wastes go into the river.

Agriculture Pesticides, sewage waste and soil carried away by water.

Sources of pollution

Equator

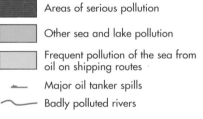

- Areas of serious pollution
- Other sea and lake pollution
- Frequent pollution of the sea from oil on shipping routes
- Major oil tanker spills
- Badly polluted rivers

Rubbish and sewage are dumped into the rivers and the sea (see the diagram above). Oil spills occur from damaged or sinking oil tankers. Plants, birds and animals in the water die as a result.

Air pollution

- Areas where rain can be very acidic
- Large cities that often have unhealthy air

Coal, oil and gas burned in power stations have sulphur and nitrogen in their smoke. This goes into the sky and it combines with rain to make acids (see the diagram on page 21). The acid kills trees and plants, and fish in the rivers and lakes.

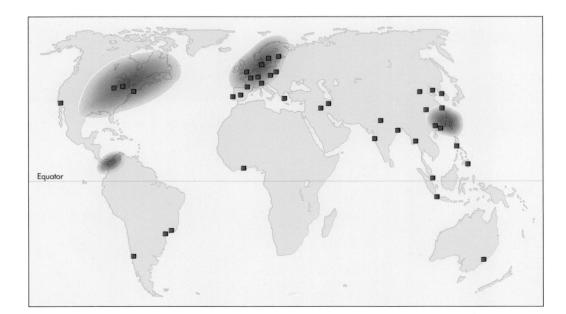

Equator

–Developed & Developing Countries–

All countries have both rich and poor people but some countries have more poor people than others. The amount of food that people have to eat and the age that they die can often depend on where they live in the world. The world can be divided into two parts – the North and the South. The richer countries are in the North and the poorer countries are in the South. The map below shows the dividing line, with Australia and New Zealand in the North. The list on the right shows some contrasts between the North and the South. Some of these contrasts can be seen in the maps on these pages.

North	South
Rich	Poor
Healthy	Poor health
Educated	Limited education
Well fed	Poorly fed
Small families	Larger families
Many industries	Fewer industries
Few farmers	Many farmers
Give aid	Receive aid

The South has over three-quarters of the world's population but less than a quarter of its wealth.

Income

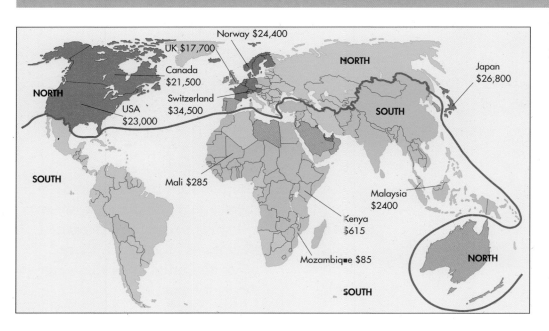

- Very rich countries
- Rich countries
- Poor countries
- Very poor countries

Norway $24,400
UK $17,700
Canada $21,500
Switzerland $34,500
USA $23,000
Japan $26,800
Mali $285
Malaysia $2400
Kenya $615
Mozambique $85

NORTH
SOUTH

The map shows how much money there is to spend on each person in a country. This is called income per person – this is worked out by dividing the wealth of a country by its population. The map gives examples of developed and developing countries.

How long do people live?

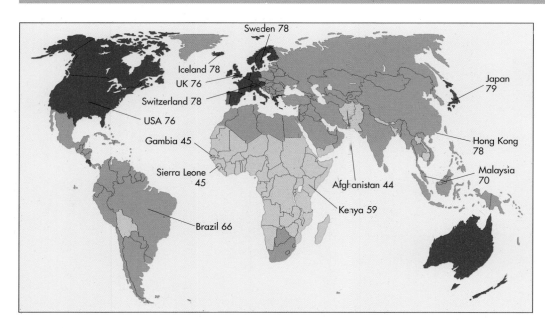

This is the average age when people die

- Over 75 years
- 60 – 75 years
- Under 60 years

Sweden 78
Iceland 78
UK 76
Switzerland 78
USA 76
Gambia 45
Sierra Leone 45
Brazil 66
Afghanistan 44
Kenya 59
Japan 79
Hong Kong 78
Malaysia 70

The average age when people die is called life expectancy. In the world, the average life expectancy is 65 years. Some of the highest and lowest ages of death are shown on the map.

Food and famine

Below the amount

Above the amount

Over a third above the amount

★ Major famines since 1980

If people do not have enough to eat they become unhealthy. This map shows where in the world people have less than and more than the amount of food they need to live a healthy life.

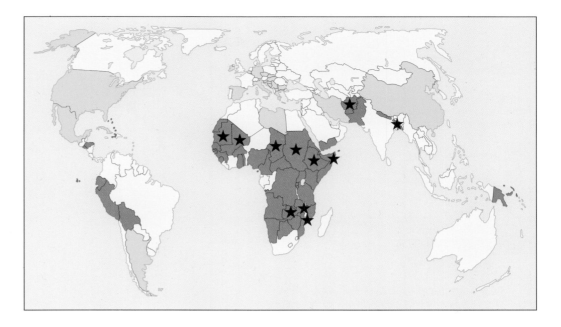

Education

Over half the adults

Between a quarter and a half of the adults

Less than a quarter of the adults

The map shows the proportion of adults in each country who cannot read or write a simple sentence. Can you think of some reasons why more people cannot read or write in some places in the world than in others?

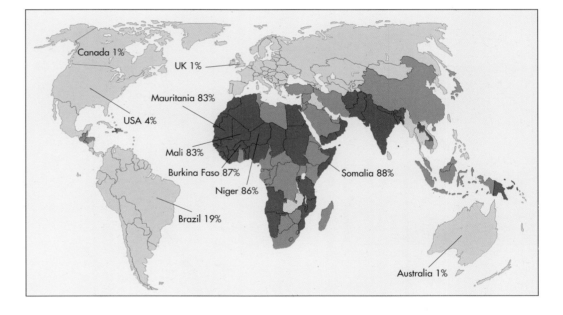

Development aid

Over $50 received per person each year

Up to $50 received per person each year

Up to $50 given per person each year

Over $50 given per person each year

Countries that receive or give no aid

Some countries receive aid from other countries. Money is one type of aid and is used to help with food, health and education problems. The map shows how much aid different countries give or receive.

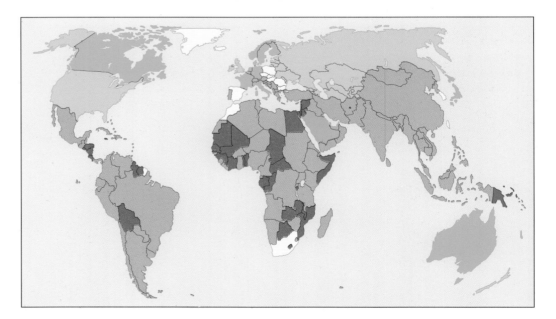

Work and Industry

What type of work?

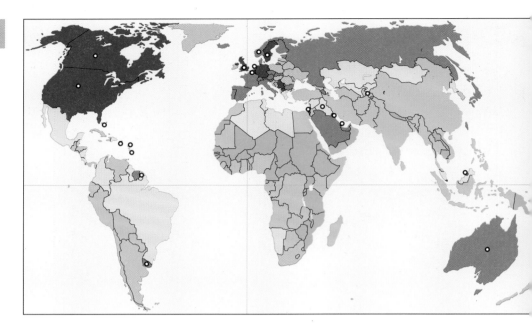

The number of workers employed in manufacturing for every 100 workers engaged in agriculture

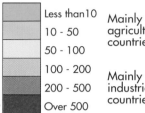

Less than 10	Mainly agricultural countries
10 - 50	
50 - 100	
100 - 200	Mainly industrial countries (manufacturing & service industries)
200 - 500	
Over 500	

○ Over two-thirds of total workforce employed in service industries (work in offices, shops, tourism, transport, construction and government)

Who makes what

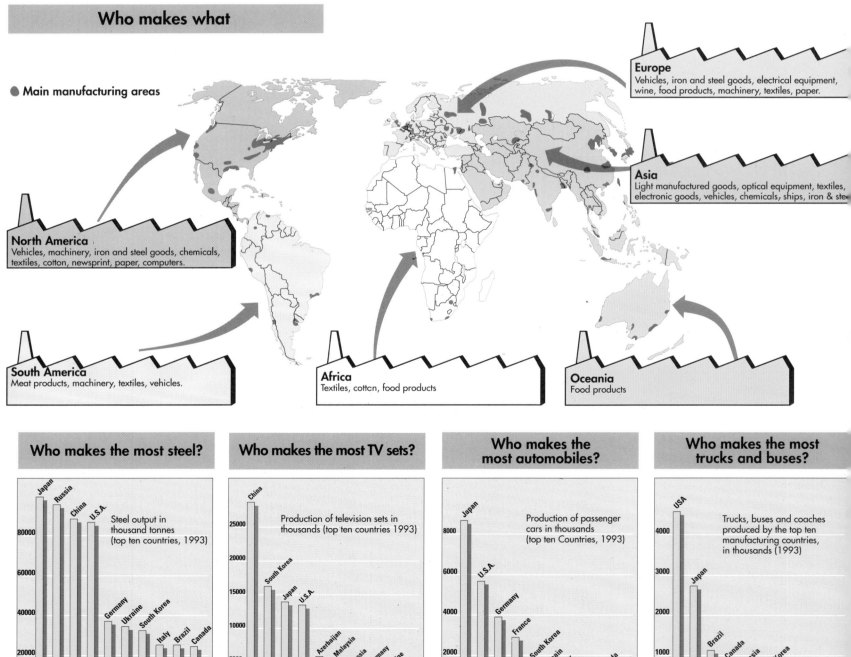

● Main manufacturing areas

Europe
Vehicles, iron and steel goods, electrical equipment, wine, food products, machinery, textiles, paper.

Asia
Light manufactured goods, optical equipment, textiles, electronic goods, vehicles, chemicals, ships, iron & ste

North America
Vehicles, machinery, iron and steel goods, chemicals, textiles, cotton, newsprint, paper, computers.

South America
Meat products, machinery, textiles, vehicles.

Africa
Textiles, cotton, food products

Oceania
Food products

Who makes the most steel?

Steel output in thousand tonnes (top ten countries, 1993)

Japan, Russia, China, U.S.A., Germany, Ukraine, South Korea, Italy, Brazil, Canada

Who makes the most TV sets?

Production of television sets in thousands (top ten countries 1993)

China, South Korea, Japan, U.S.A., Azerbaijan, Malaysia, Russia, Germany, Ukraine, Brazil

Who makes the most automobiles?

Production of passenger cars in thousands (top ten Countries, 1993)

Japan, U.S.A., Germany, France, South Korea, Spain, U.K., Italy, Canada, Russia

Who makes the most trucks and buses?

Trucks, buses and coaches produced by the top ten manufacturing countries, in thousands (1993)

USA, Japan, Brazil, Canada, Russia, South Korea, France, Thailand, Germany, UK

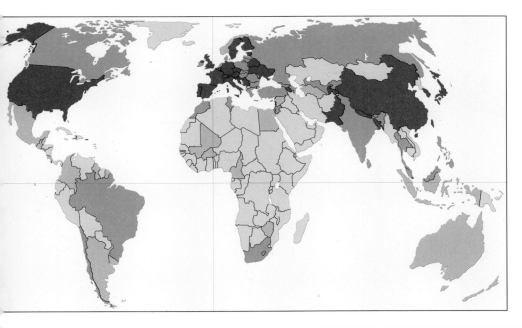

Manufactured goods (including machinery, automobiles, trucks and airplanes) as a percentage of total exports for 1993

	Over 75%
	50 - 75%
	25 - 50%
	Under 25%

As a general rule, countries prefer to export manufactured goods rather than raw materials. Manufactured goods tend to be more valuable and create more wealth for a country. The amount and type of goods a country exports help to show the level of development, education, and technology in that country.

World trade

rcentage share of total world
oorts by value 1995

	Over 10% of world trade
	5 - 10% of world trade
	1 - 5% of world trade
	Under 1% of world trade

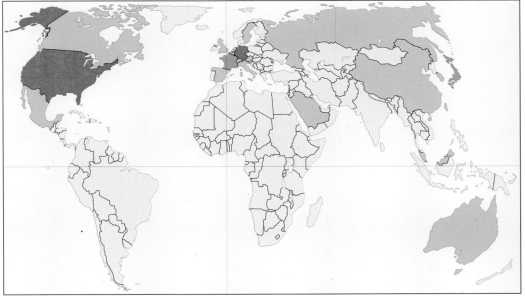

you compare this map with the one on
ge 80 you will notice that countries which
ly on agriculture as their main industry do
ot have a large share of world trade. These
untries tend not to export manufactured
ods which have a high value.

Workers in the labour force

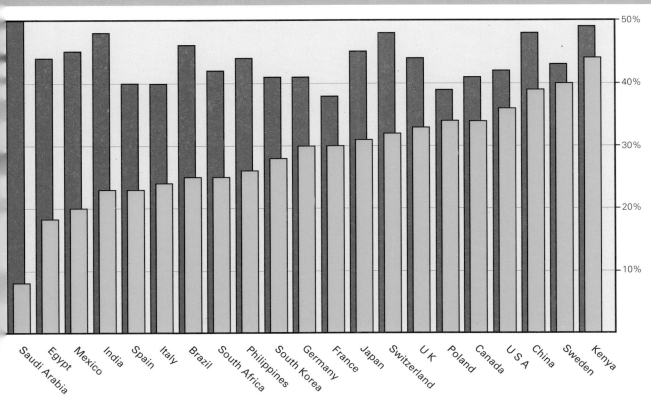

Workers as a percentage of the total (male and female) population aged 15 – 64 years

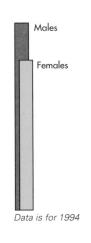

Males

Females

Data is for 1994

CARTOGRAPHY BY PHILIP'S. COPYRIGHT GEORGE PHILIP LTD

World Languages

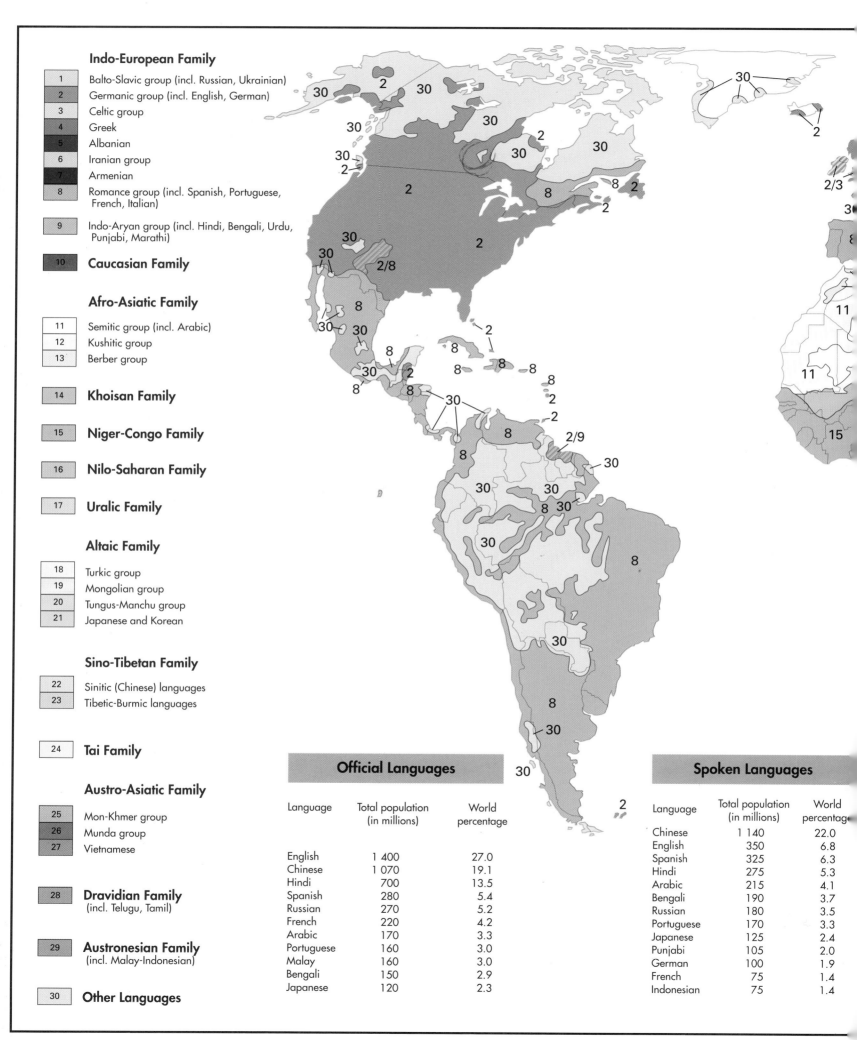

Indo-European Family

1	Balto-Slavic group (incl. Russian, Ukrainian)
2	Germanic group (incl. English, German)
3	Celtic group
4	Greek
5	Albanian
6	Iranian group
7	Armenian
8	Romance group (incl. Spanish, Portuguese, French, Italian)
9	Indo-Aryan group (incl. Hindi, Bengali, Urdu, Punjabi, Marathi)

10 Caucasian Family

Afro-Asiatic Family

11	Semitic group (incl. Arabic)
12	Kushitic group
13	Berber group

14 Khoisan Family

15 Niger-Congo Family

16 Nilo-Saharan Family

17 Uralic Family

Altaic Family

18	Turkic group
19	Mongolian group
20	Tungus-Manchu group
21	Japanese and Korean

Sino-Tibetan Family

22	Sinitic (Chinese) languages
23	Tibetic-Burmic languages

24 Tai Family

Austro-Asiatic Family

25	Mon-Khmer group
26	Munda group
27	Vietnamese

28 Dravidian Family
(incl. Telugu, Tamil)

29 Austronesian Family
(incl. Malay-Indonesian)

30 Other Languages

Official Languages

Language	Total population (in millions)	World percentage
English	1 400	27.0
Chinese	1 070	19.1
Hindi	700	13.5
Spanish	280	5.4
Russian	270	5.2
French	220	4.2
Arabic	170	3.3
Portuguese	160	3.0
Malay	160	3.0
Bengali	150	2.9
Japanese	120	2.3

Spoken Languages

Language	Total population (in millions)	World percentage
Chinese	1 140	22.0
English	350	6.8
Spanish	325	6.3
Hindi	275	5.3
Arabic	215	4.1
Bengali	190	3.7
Russian	180	3.5
Portuguese	170	3.3
Japanese	125	2.4
Punjabi	105	2.0
German	100	1.9
French	75	1.4
Indonesian	75	1.4

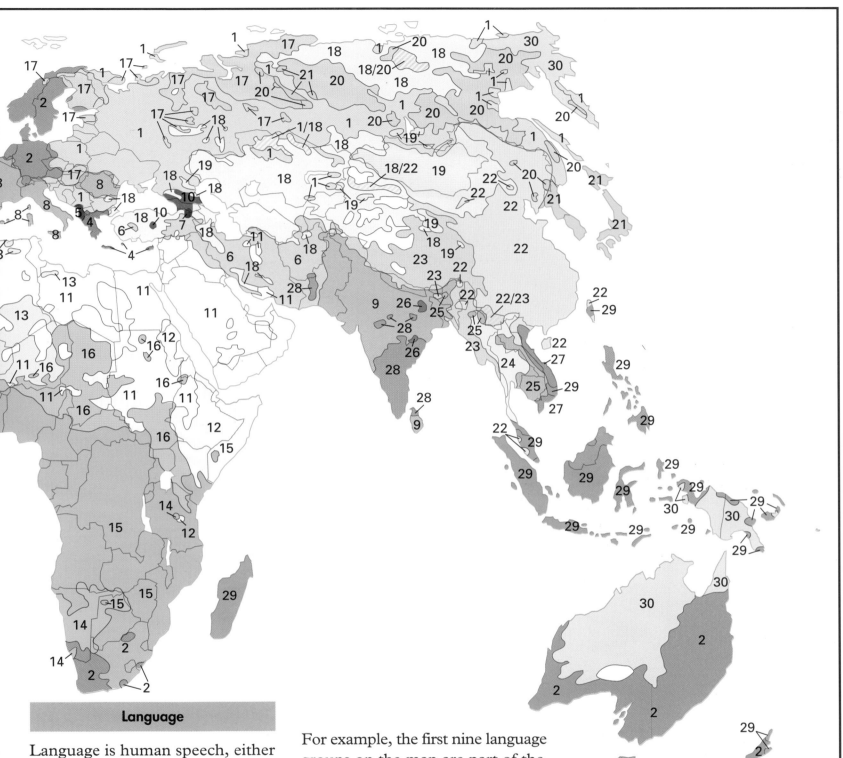

Language

Language is human speech, either spoken or written. It makes it possible for people to talk to other people and to write their thoughts and ideas.

Language Families

Each family is made up of groups of similar languages. They are thought to have developed from common parent languages.

For example, the first nine language groups on the map are part of the Indo-European language family. About half the people in the world speak languages in this family. English and German are Germanic languages.

French, Italian, Spanish, and Portuguese are Romance languages. Russian is a Slavic language. Bengali and Hindustani are Indo-Aryan languages. Speakers of all these languages once lived in an area extending from Northern India to Western Europe. Now, they live in other parts of the world. The Sino-Tibetan family is the next largest. This family includes Chinese which has about half a dozen dialects.

World Statistics
Agriculture

Land Use

Major categories of land use are shown as circles and the size of the circle is in proportion to its land area. Arable land includes permanent crops such as coffee and rubber. Other land use types include built-up areas, roads and waste lands such as high mountains.

Continent/region	land area	arable and cropland	permanent grassland	forest and woodland	other land use
Africa	29 635	6	30	24	40
Asia	30 862	17	34	18	31
Europe	5 715	32	16	32	20
North America	21 370	13	17	41	30
Australia and Oceania	8 453	6	51	23	20
South America	17 529	26	28	48	18
Russia	16 889	8	5	45	42
World	**130 454**	**11**	**26**	**32**	**31**

thousand square kilometres   *% of continent or region land area*

Russia is in both Europe and Asia and so is shown separately.

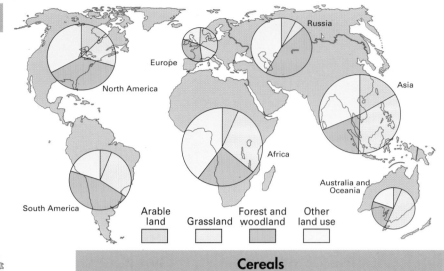

Arable land   Grassland   Forest and woodland   Other land use

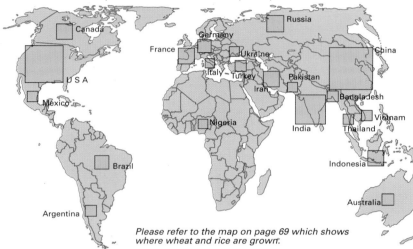

Please refer to the map on page 69 which shows where wheat and rice are grown.

Cereals

The map and table show the total production of wheat, maize and rice in millions of tonnes for each country. The size of the squares is in proportion to the production of leading cereals in the countries shown.

Country	Cereal	% of World
China	436	21
USA	338	17
India	214	10
Russia	68	3.3
France	63	3.1
Indonesia	60	2.9
Iran	60	2.9
Canada	59	2.9
Brazil	46	2.2
Germany	42	2.0
Australia	34	1.7

Country	Cereal	% of World
Argentina	30	1.5
Bangladesh	29	1.4
Turkey	29	1.4
Mexico	27	1.3
Vietnam	27	1.3
Thailand	26	1.3
Pakistan	24	1.2
Ukraine	24	1.2
Nigeria	22	1.1
Italy	21	1.0
World	**2 050**	**100**

Livestock

The map and table show the total number of cattle, sheep and pigs in each country. The size of the squares is in proportion to the number of livestock.

Country	million head	% of World total
China	643	19.7
India	252	7.7
Brazil	210	6.4
USA	172	5.2
Australia	152	4.7
Russia	96	2.9
Argentina	78	2.4
Iran	59	1.8
New Zealand	59	1.8
Mexico	59	1.8
Ethiopia	51	1.6

Country	million head	% of World total
UK	49	1.5
Pakistan	49	1.5
Turkey	48	1.5
Spain	46	1.4
France	45	1.4
Sudan	45	1.4
South Africa	43	1.3
Kazakstan	36	1.1
Colombia	31	1.0
Poland	28	0.9
World	**3 269**	**100**

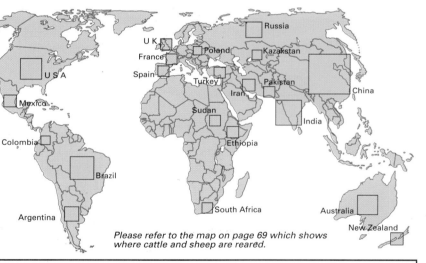

Please refer to the map on page 69 which shows where cattle and sheep are reared.

Fish

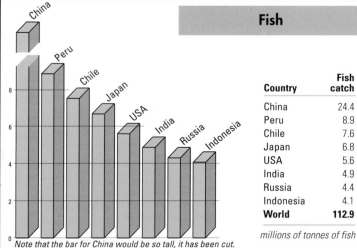

Country	Fish catch
China	24.4
Peru	8.9
Chile	7.6
Japan	6.8
USA	5.6
India	4.9
Russia	4.4
Indonesia	4.1
World	**112.9**

millions of tonnes of fish

Note that the bar for China would be so tall, it has been cut.

Timber

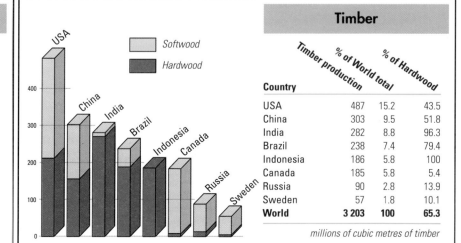

Softwood   Hardwood

Country	Timber production	% of World total	% of Hardwood
USA	487	15.2	43.5
China	303	9.5	51.8
India	282	8.8	96.3
Brazil	238	7.4	79.4
Indonesia	186	5.8	100
Canada	185	5.8	5.4
Russia	90	2.8	13.9
Sweden	57	1.8	10.1
World	**3 203**	**100**	**65.3**

millions of cubic metres of timber

World Statistics
Minerals and Energy

Minerals

Iron ore

Country	Production (million tonnes)	% of World total
China	153	15
Brazil	121	12
Australia	91	9
Russia	44	4
India	42	4
USA	39	4
Ukraine	29	3
Canada	21	2
South Africa	21	2
Venezuela	15	1
Others	444	44
World 1994	**1 020**	**100**

Copper ore

Country	Production (thousand tonnes)	% of World total
Chile	2 506	25
USA	1 850	18
Canada	724	7
Russia	590	6
Indonesia	479	5
China	396	4
Poland	384	4
Australia	365	4
Mexico	360	4
Peru	360	4
Others	2 036	19
World 1994	**10 050**	**100**

Steel

Country	Production (million tonnes)	% of World total
Japan	102	14
China	94	13
USA	94	13
Russia	49	7
Germany	42	6
South Korea	37	5
Canada	28	4
Italy	28	4
Brazil	25	3
Ukraine	22	3
Others	229	28
World 1994	**750**	**100**

Aluminium ore (Bauxite)

Country	Production (million tonnes)	% of World total
Australia	42	38
Guinea	14	13
Jamaica	11	10
Brazil	10	9
China	7	6
Venezuela	5	5
India	5	5
Surinam	4	3
Guyana	2	2
Greece	2	2
Others	10	7
World 1994	**112**	**100**

Gold

Country	Production (tonnes)	% of World total
South Africa	522	23
USA	330	15
Australia	254	11
Canada	150	7
Russia	142	6
China	136	6
Indonesia	74	3
Brazil	67	3
Uzbekistan	64	3
Papua New Guinea	55	2
Others	481	21
World 1994	**2 275**	**100**

Refined Aluminium

Country	Production (million tonnes)	% of World total
USA	7	25
Russia	3	10
Canada	2	9
China	2	6
Australia	1	5
Brazil	1	5
Japan	1	5
Germany	1	4
Norway	0.9	3
Venezuela	0.7	2
Others	7.4	26
World 1994	**27**	**100**

Energy

Coal

Country	Production (million tonnes)	% of World total
China	1 298	28
USA	937	20
India	288	6
Russia	262	6
Germany	246	5
Australia	241	5
South Africa	206	4
Poland	201	4
Ukraine	84	2
Kazakstan	83	2
Others	774	18
World 1994	**4 620**	**100**

Crude oil

Country	Production (million tonnes)	% of World total
Saudi Arabia	429	13
USA	383	11
Russia	301	9
Iran	183	5
Mexico	164	5
Venezuela	162	5
China	159	5
Norway	156	5
UK	130	4
United Arab Em.	117	3
Others	1178	35
World 1994	**3 362**	**100**

Natural gas

Country	Production (billion metres^3)	% of World total
Russia	572	25
USA	557	25
Canada	156	7
UK	86	4
Netherlands	77	3
Indonesia	68	3
Algeria	67	3
Uzbekistan	47	2
Saudi Arabia	42	2
Norway	42	2
Others	559	24
World 1994	**2 273**	**100**

Hydro-electricity

Country	Production (billion kilowatt hours)	% of World total
Canada	328	14
USA	282	12
Brazil	243	10
Russia	177	7
China	168	7
Norway	113	5
France	81	3
Japan	76	3
India	71	3
Sweden	59	2
Others	805	34
World 1994	**2 403**	**100**

Energy use and its origins

equivalent of million tonnes of oil	1994 Production	% of World total	Energy source				
			Solids	Gases	Liquids	Hydro	Tradi- tional
World	8 473	100	28	33	22	10	7
Africa	357	4	21	25	12	2	39
Asia	2 693	32	39	31	13	6	10
Aust. & Oceania	118	1	38	36	17	4	6
Europe	2 429	29	23	31	30	14	2
North America	2 538	30	23	38	26	11	2
South America	336	4	6	41	19	12	23

Electricity production

	1994 Production	% of World total	% of total electricity made by-		
			thermal	hydro	nuclear
USA	3 268	26	71	9	20
Japan	964	8	64	8	28
China	928	7	80	19	2
Russia	876	7	69	20	11
Canada	554	4	21	59	19
Germany	528	4	67	4	29
France	475	4	7	17	76
India	384	3	80	18	1
UK	325	3	71	2	27
Brazil	261	2	7	93	0
World	**12 680**	**100**	**63**	**19**	**17**

thousand million kilowatt hours

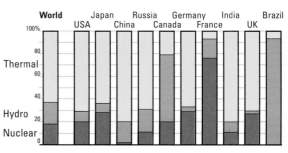

Population

Urban and Rural Population

The bars and the data show the breakdown of the world population into urban (people that live in towns and cities) and rural (people who live in the country) populations. The figures are for 1975 and estimates of what is likely in the years 2000 and 2025. Russia is included in Europe.

Continent	Urban population percentage		
	1975	2000	2025
Africa	25	37	54
Asia	25	38	55
Europe	67	75	83
Latin America	61	77	85
North America	74	77	85
Australia and Oceania	72	70	75
World	**38**	**48**	**61**

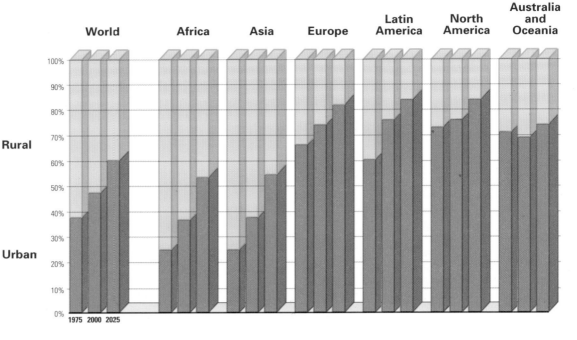

Age Groups

The circles on this map represent the population of the continents. Their area is drawn in proportion to their total population. The colours show the proportion that is in each age group. See the figures in the table below.

- over 65 years
- 15 - 64 years
- under 15 years

Continent	under 15	15-64	over 64
Africa	44	53	3
Asia	32	63	5
Europe	19	67	14
Latin America	34	61	5
North America	22	65	12
Australia and Oceania	26	64	9
World	**32**	**62**	**6**

Canadian Immigration

In 1996 the total population of Canada was 29 784 000. Of these, 4 971 000 had been born outside of Canada (17 % of the population). The data shows the regions of the World where the immigrants came from. The size of the circle represents the number of people emigrating to Canada from that region.

Birthplace	Number	% of immigrants
Total	**4 971 000**	**100**
Europe	**2 332 000**	**47**
Southern Europe	714 000	14
UK	656 000	13
N. & W. Europe	514 000	10
Eastern Europe	448 000	9
Asia	**1 563 000**	**31**
Eastern Asia	589 000	12
S.E. Asia	409 000	8
Southern Asia	354 000	7
S.W. Asia	211 000	4
Americas	**798 000**	**16**
Caribbean	279 000	6
Central & S. America	274 000	6
USA	245 000	5
Africa	**229 000**	**5**
Australia and Oceania	**49 000**	**1**

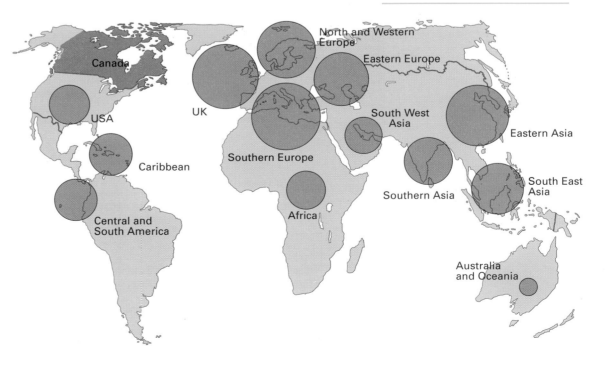

World Statistics
Quality of Life

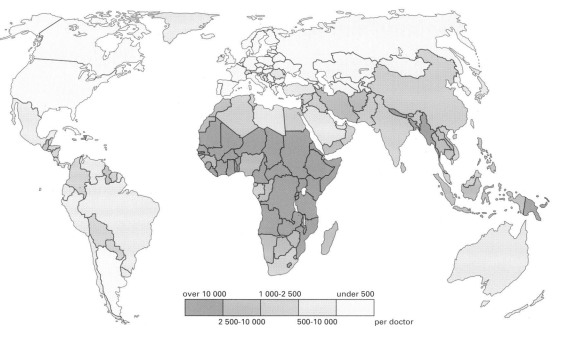

Doctors

The countries on the map show the number of people per doctor in each country.

Country	people per doctor	Country	people per doctor
Italy	207	China	1 063
Russia	222	Mauritius	1 165
UK	300	Egypt	1 316
Norway	308	Vietnam	2 279
France	334	India	2 459
Germany	367	Nigeria	5 208
Sweden	394	Sudan	10 000
USA	421	Burma	12 528
Canada	464	Bangladesh	12 884
Australia	500	Kenya	21 970
Romania	538	Chad	30 030
Japan	608	Mozambique	36 225
Saudi Arabia	749		

Please also refer to the map on page 78 which shows life expectancy.

over 10 000		1 000-2 500		under 500
	2 500-10 000		500-10 000	per doctor

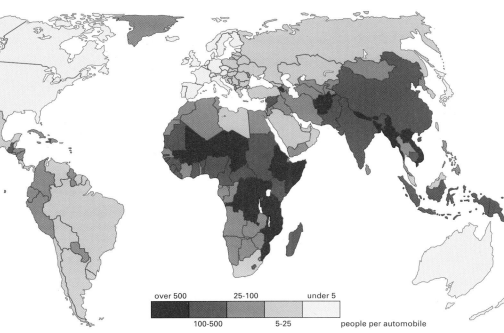

Automobiles

The countries on the map show the number of people for each automobile in the country. Trucks are excluded. For example, in Canada there are 14.3 million automobiles and a population of 30.2 million. There are 2.1 people per automobile.

Country	people per automobile	Country	people per automobile
Mozambique	1 910	Russia	14
Bangladesh	1 592	Brazil	13
Vietnam	749	Mexico	12
Tanzania	650	Saudi Arabia	11
China	346	South Africa	11
India	284	Argentina	8
Sudan	267	Taiwan	6
Kenya	203	Japan	3
Nigeria	153	UK	3
Egypt	54	France	2
Iran	45	Canada	2
Zimbabwe	39	USA	2
Chile	18		

over 500		25-100		under 5
	100-500		5-25	people per automobile

Telephones

The countries on the map show how many telephone lines there are per 1 000 people in each country.

Country	Telephone lines	Country	Telephone lines
Sweden	681	Germany	501
USA	627	Greece	500
Denmark	613	Japan	487
Switzerland	612	New Zealand	479
Canada	590	Singapore	478
France	558	Austria	465
Norway	556	Belgium	457
Iceland	554		
Finland	550	Tanzania	3
Luxembourg	537	Madagascar	2
Netherlands	525	Uganda	2
Australia	510	Cambodia	1
UK	502	Liberia	1

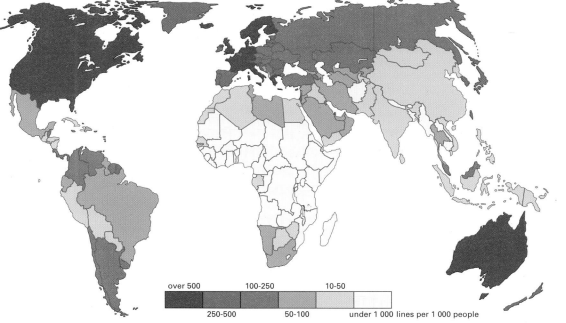

over 500		100-250		10-50
	250-500		50-100	under 1 000 lines per 1 000 people

Canada's Foreign Trade

This map shows circles which represent the value of Canada's trade with the countries named. The size of the circle varies according to the amount of trade. Trade means the value of the exports and imports added together. The data is listed in the table on the right. The values are in million $. The list is in the order of the value of trade with Canada for each particular country.

Country	Trade total	% of total	Country	Trade total	% of total	Country	Trade total	% of total	Country	Trade total	% of total
USA	383 488	73.7	France	5 431	1.0	Thailand	1 700	0.3	South Africa	863	0.2
Japan	25 614	4.9	Norway	3 306	0.6	Venezuela	1 540	0.3	Colombia	80	0.2
UK	9 964	1.9	Belgium	2 805	0.5	Spain	1 422	0.3	Russia	756	0.1
China	8 592	1.7	Netherlands	2 799	0.5	Indonesia	1 333	0.3	Chile	712	0.1
Germany	8 575	1.6	Australia	2 699	0.5	Saudi Arabia	1 095	0.2	Cuba	637	0.1
Mexico	6 939	1.3	Brazil	2 498	0.5	India	1 045	0.2	Nigeria	627	0.1
Korea	6 318	1.2	Malaysia	2 271	0.4	Austria	890	0.2	Iran	583	0.1
Italy	5 463	1.1	Singapore	1 923	0.4	Philippines	876	0.2	New Zealand	518	0.1

Type of Goods Traded with Canada

These bar graphs show the two parts of Canada's trade, the imports (goods coming into the country) and exports (goods going out of the country).

Exports $ 280.6 billion

Imports $ 239.6 billion

Type	Exports	Imports
Agricultural and fishing products	9%	6%
Energy products	9%	4%
Forestry products	12%	1%
Industrial goods and materials	19%	8%
		32%
Machinery and equipment	22%	21%
Transport products	23%	11%
Consumer goods		17%
Other types of goods	3% / 3%	

Importance of Trade

The colour of the country on the map shows how important exporting is to the wealth of the country. The value of the exports are shown as a percentage of the country's total wealth. Some sample figures are shown in the table above the map. The values are in billion $US. The figures are the value of exports as a percentage of the wealth of the country (the Gross National Product).

Country	Exports/Wealth	Country	Exports/Wealth	Country	Exports/Wealth	Country	Exports/Wealth	Country	Exports/Wealth
Singapore	148	Finland	38	Switzerland	27	Tanzania	18	Cuba	12
Malaysia	94	Nigeria	35	Ecuador	27	Iraq	18	India	10
Ireland	85	Canada	34	Russia	24	Spain	17	Japan	9
Gabon	72	Saudi Arabia	32	Algeria	23	Morocco	16	USA	8
Angola	72	Denmark	31	Germany	23	Australia	16	Brazil	8
Czech Republic	54	Norway	31	U K	22	Mexico	15	Egypt	8
Netherlands	53	Sri Lanka	30	South Africa	21	Colombia	14	Argentina	8
Trinidad	51	Hungary	30	China	20	Ukraine	14	Iran	6
Taiwan	44	Vietnam	29	France	20	Pakistan	13	Sudan	3
Sweden	38	Venezuela	28	Bolivia	19	Turkey	13	Burma	2

World Exports

The pie-diagram and the data below show the type of goods that make up the total exports of all the countries in the World.

- Other goods 2%
- Food, beverages and tobacco 9%
- Crude materials (excluding fuels) 5%
- Fuels 8%
- Chemicals 10%
- Trucks and automobiles 5%
- Machinery and transport equipment 32%
- Metal manufactured goods 7%
- Other manufactures 22%

Total value : 4 229 billion US$

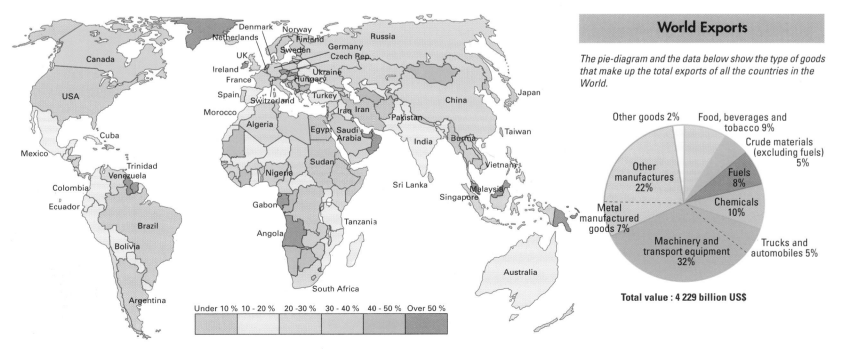

Under 10 % 10 - 20 % 20 -30 % 30 - 40 % 40 - 50 % Over 50 %

World Statistics
The Environment

Protected areas

The data below shows a selection of the countries with large areas of protected land. The map also shows countries that have over 100 000 sq. km of protected land. Canada has 9% and over 800 000 sq. km. The map shows how much of the total land of the country is protected from use by humans and is left to the plants and animals.

Country	% of country protected	Country	% of country protected
Ecuador	40	Chile	18
Denmark	33	Norway	18
Venezuela	30	Panama	18
Germany	26	Cambodia	17
Austria	25	Tanzania	16
New Zealand	23	Israel	15
Dominican Rep.	22	USA	14
Slovak Rep.	21	Czech Rep.	14
UK	21	Thailand	14
Botswana	19	Rwanda	13
Switzerland	19		

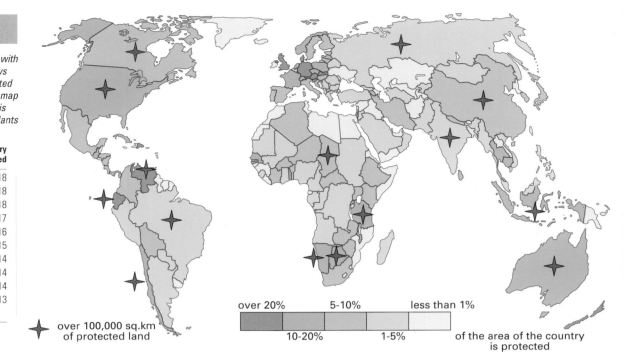

✦ over 100,000 sq.km of protected land

over 20%   5-10%   less than 1%
10-20%   1-5%
of the area of the country is protected

Safe water

Most industrialized countries have safe water in rural as well as urban areas. Below are some of the figures for countries that have contaminated water supplies, a major factor in the poor health of such nations. The map and table show the percentage of the population who have water that is clean and safe to drink.

Country	% of population with safe water	Country	% of population with safe water
Tanzania	38	Swaziland	30
Uganda	38	Madagascar	29
Malawi	37	Haiti	28
Mali	37	Papua New Guinea	28
Somalia	37	Zambia	27
Cambodia	37	Ethiopia	25
Vietnam	36	Chad	24
Congo	34	Bhutan	21
Sierra Leone	34	Central African Rep.	18
Mozambique	33	Afghanistan	12
Angola	32		

100%   50-75%
75-100%   less than 50% of the people have safe water

Carbon Dioxide

Large quantities of carbon dioxide are produced when coal, oil and gas are burnt to make electricity. Carbon dioxide is thought to be a gas which is changing the climate of the world, one of the 'greenhouse gases'. The data shows some of the greatest producers of these emissions.

Country	Tonnes per year per person	Country	Tonnes per year per person
United Arab Em.	34	Saudi Arabia	13
USA	19	Ukraine	12
Singapore	18	North Korea	11
Kazakstan	18	Kuwait	11
Trinidad	17	Germany	11
Australia	15	Turkmenistan	11
Canada	14	Denmark	10
Norway	14	Belgium	10
Russia	14	Belarus	10
Estonia	14	UK	10
Czech Rep.	13		

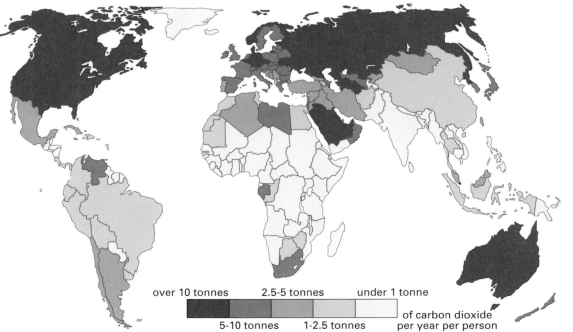

over 10 tonnes   2.5-5 tonnes   under 1 tonne
5-10 tonnes   1-2.5 tonnes
of carbon dioxide per year per person

Glossary

Agriculture: Managing the land and the soil in order to grow crops or graze livestock upon it.

Aid: Resources given to less-developed countries, usually to promote development or to relieve suffering.

Atmosphere: The layer of air which surrounds the Earth and supports life.

Biosphere: The area of the Earth's crust and its atmosphere in which life is found.

Census: A survey to count the number of people in a country, and to find out more about them.

Climate: Long term patterns of weather conditions of an area.

Confluence: The point where two or more streams come together, forming a larger stream or river.

Conservation: The careful and thoughtful use of the Earth's resources.

Continent: One of the Earth's seven large land masses.

Continental drift: The slow shifting of the continents on the surface of the Earth, caused by the movement of the underlying plates.

Contour: A line on a map which joins all places of equal height above sea level.

Cross-section: A side-view showing the internal structure of an area of land.

Deforestation: The cutting down of trees, usually to clear the land for another use, such as agriculture or road building.

Delta: A shallow area formed at the mouth of a river when sediment is deposited to form large mud banks.

Demography: The study of human populations.

Deposition: The laying down of material that has been previously eroded and transported by rivers, ice or wind.

Desert: A region with a dry climate and little or no vegetation.

Desertification: The spread of desert conditions into areas which formerly had vegetation.

Developed countries: Industrial countries in which many people live in towns and cities and enjoy a high standard of living.

Developing countries: Poorer countries in which agriculture remains the main activity, but where people are beginning to enjoy a better standard of living.

Earthquake: A shaking of the Earth's crust caused by a movement of rock below the surface.

Ecosystem: The relationship among plants, animals and the environment in which they live.

El Niño: A warm Pacific ocean current which periodically replaces cold currents, causing unusual weather conditions over a wide area.

Emigrants: People who leave one country, or region, to settle in another.

Environment: The surroundings within which human beings, animals and plants live.

Erosion: The wearing away of the Earth's surface, mainly by water (rivers, ice and the sea) and wind.

Exports: Goods that are produced in one country and sent to another for use or resale.

Estuary: The mouth of a river where it widens and flows into a sea or ocean.

Famine: An extreme and widespread shortage of food.

Forestry: The planting, cultivating and harvesting of woodland to provide timber for sale.

Flood plain: A lowland alongside a river which has been built up by material deposited during floods.

Geography: The study of the Earth and the ways that human beings interact with it.

Geothermal: The heat of the Earth's interior.

Glacier: A mass of ice which slowly flows down a valley under its own weight.

Global warming: A slow increase in world temperatures that may be caused by human activities such as coal burning.

Green belt: Areas of parks, farmland, or uncultivated land surrounding communities.

Gross domestic product (GDP): The total value of goods and services produced by a country during a year.

Hurricane: A very powerful tropical storm, capable of causing widespread damage.

Hydroelectric power: Electricity produced from a natural or artificial flow of moving water.

Ice-sheet: A large area of snow and ice covering a land mass; for example, Antarctica.

Immigrants: Settlers from another country or region.

Imports: Goods that are brought into a country and sold to its inhabitants.

Irrigation: An artificial way to supply water to an area in which there is a shortage for growing crops.

Isthmus: A narrow strip of land, with water on either side, which connects two large areas of land.

Landform: Any natural feature of the Earth's surface, such as a hill or a valley.

Land use: The use of land by human activities, such as agriculture, industry or forestry.

Lava: Molten rock which reaches the Earth's surface after being pushed upwards by volcanic activity.

Map projection: A way of representing the curved surface of the Earth on a flat sheet of paper.

Manufacturing industry: Using raw materials and machines to make finished products.

Meander: A bend in a river, caused by erosion on the side that the river flows fastest.

Migration: The movement of people from one place to another, as they search for better opportunities.

Monsoon: Seasonal winds in Asia that bring wet weather in summer and dry weather in winter.

Moraine: An accumulation of boulders, stones, or other debris carried and deposited by a glacier.

National park: A special area of land set aside to preserve wildlife and natural beauty where development is controlled by government agencies.

Nuclear power: A way of creating electricity by using nuclear fuel.

Overpopulation: When a region or country has too many people for the available resources.

Ozone layer: A layer of ozone gas high above the Earth that blocks out the Sun's harmful radiation.

Pasture: An area of grassland suitable for grazing by animals.

Peninsula: A narrow strip of land that juts into the sea.

Permafrost: Band of permanently frozen subsoil occurring throughout the Polar Regions and locally in perenially frigid areas.

Plateau: An elevated area of land which is fairly flat, although it may be broken by deep river valleys.

Pollution: Damage to the natural environment caused by the activities of human beings.

Precipitation: Any form of condensation in the atmosphere, like rain, hail or snow.

Primary Industry: Activities providing goods which have not been processed or changed, such as mining.

Rainforest: Dense forest growing in tropical regions that have very heavy rainfall throughout the year.

Reforestation: The planting of trees in an area which has been deforested in the past.

Refugees: People fleeing from their home countries because of war, persecution or poverty.

Resources: Features of the environment that are valuable to human beings. They can be renewable, such as rainfall and solar power, or nonrenewable, like coal.

Savanna: Tropical grassland found between the tropical forests and the major desert regions.

Scale: A measurement on a map that represents a certain distance on the Earth's surface.

Secondary industry: Activities producing consumer goods from basic manufactured products.

Sediment: Very small pieces of rock which have been eroded and transported by rivers, ice or wind.

Seismograph: An instrument that measures the strength and direction of earthquakes.

Shanty town: Poor-quality housing in a town or section of a town.

Solar power: Energy derived from the sun's radiation.

Staple diet: The basic foodstuff eaten in a region.

Steppe: Areas of temperate grassland, usually very flat and open.

Suburb: A built-up area on the outskirts of a city.

Summer time: System by which clocks are altered to save daylight.

Temperate: Mid-latitude regions that experience a moderate climate.

Tertiary industry: Activities that provide a service to people, such as banking, teaching and government.

Topography: The features, both natural and human-made, of a landscape.

Tornado: A small, but violent whirlwind which occurs in continental land masses.

Transpiration: The process by which plants give off and lose water vapour.

Tree line: The line on a mountain above which trees do not grow because of the polar-like climatic conditions.

Tributary: A stream or river which flows into a larger river.

Tropical: The area of the Earth found between the Tropic of Cancer and the Tropic of Capricorn, experiencing hot, often humid, weather conditions.

Tsunami: Large, destructive waves caused by underwater earthquakes or volcanic eruptions.

Tundra: A vast treeless zone that lies between the Arctic ice and the northern forested regions.

Underpopulation: Too few people in an area to fully develop the potential resources there.

Underdeveloped countries: A term applied to poor countries with few industries

Urban areas: Built-up towns or cities in which many people live close together.

Urbanization: The growth and expansion of urban areas.

Valley: A long depression which is lower than the surrounding land.

Vegetation: The plant life of a particular area.

Volcano: An opening in the Earth's crust through which lava and steam may periodically erupt.

Weathering: The erosion of rocks caused by the effects of weather.

Index

The names in the index are in alphabetical order. If a name on a map has a description, *Lake Winnipeg* for example, then the index entry will be *Winnipeg, Lake*. If the same name refers to places in different countries, then the country names are given in brackets, for example, *Kingston (Canada)* and *Kingston (Jamaica)*.

To find a place on the map, first, find the name in the index. The bold number after the placename is the map page number. After the page number there is a letter and another number. The letter shows you the column, the number, and the row, on that particular map page. These letters and numbers appear around the edges of the map. The place name is in the square at the intersection of the particular column and row. If a name goes across from one square to another the square reference is to where the name begins.

In the index, all names, except city and town names are followed by a descriptive word. This will be in the form of the name shown on the map, *Ontario*, *Orange*, or *Oman*, for example, followed by a descriptive word such as *province*, *river* or *country*. Former names of some famous places are referenced to the new name, for example, *Bombay = Mumbai*.

elyuskin, Cape 41 B11	Corsica, island 37 N11	Drava, river 39 G2	Flores, island 45 L7	Gran Chaco, region 28 E6	Hamburg 36 P6
emnitz 36 P7	Costa Brava 38 D3	Dresden 36 Q7	Florida, state 25 K5	Gran Sasso, mountain 38 F3	Hamersley Range 31 B4
engdu 45 J3	Costa del Sol, region 38 C4	Dublin 36 E6	Florida Keys 23 K6	Granada 37 F14	Hamilton (Bermuda) 27 M1
ennai 44 G5	Costa Rica, country 26 G5	Dubrovnik 39 G3	Florida Strait 23 K6	Grand Bahama Island 27 J2	Hamilton (Canada) 23 K2
erbourg 37 H8	Coteau du Missouri, Plateau du 22 F1	Duero, river 37 G12	Floro 36 L2	Grand Banks 19 N4	Hangzhou 45 K4
ernobyl 39 J1	Crete, island 39 H4	Duluth 23 H1	Fly, river 31 E2	Grand Canyon 22 D3	Hanoi 45 J4
erskiy Range 41 C14	Crimea, region 39 K2	Dundee 36 G4	Formentera, island 37 J13	Grand Cayman, island 27 H4	Hanover 36 N6
esapeake Bay 23 L3	Croatia, country 39 G2	Dunedin 31 G12	Fort Worth 23 G4	Grande Prairie 18 G3	Happy Valley-Goose Bay 19 M3
esterfield Islands F4	Crozet Islands 13 M5	Durango 26 D3	Fort-de-France 27 M5	Graz 39 G2	Harare 33 F7
eyenne 22 E2	Cuba, country 27 H3	Durban 33 G9	Fortaleza 29 H4	Great Australian Bight 31 C5	Harbin 45 L2
ba 46 C3	Cubango, river 32 E7	Dushanbe 40 F7	Foxe Basin 19 L2	Great Barrier Reef 31 E3	Harrisburg 23 L2
cago 23 J2	Culiacan 26 C3	Düsseldorf 36 L7	France, country 38 J9	Great Basin 22 C2	Hartford 23 M2
clayo 29 D4	Cumberland Plateau 23 J4	Dvina, North, river 40 C5	Frankfort 23 K3	Great Bear Lake 18 F2	Hatteras, Cape 23 L3
coutimi 19 L4	Cumberland, river 23 J3	Dzungaria, region 45 G2	Frankfurt 36 N7	Great Britain, island 34 H4	Havana 27 H3
dley, Cape 19 M2	Curitiba 29 G6		Franz Josef Land 40 B5	Great Dividing Range 31 E3	Hawaii 22 R9
engmai 45 H5	Cuzco 29 D5	East China Sea 45 L4	Fraser, river 18 F3	Great Falls 22 D1	Hawaii, state 24 Q8
huahua 26 C2	Cyprus, country 39 K4	East Indies, region 45 K7	Fredericton 19 M4	Great Khingan Mountains 45 K2	Hawaiian Islands 22 R9
le, country 29 D6	Czech Republic, country 38 F2	East London 33 F9	Freetown 33 B5	Great Plains, region 16 H3	Hay River 18 G2
mkent 40 E7		East Siberian Sea 41 B16	Freiburg 37 M8	Great Rift Valley 32 G6	Hebrides, islands 36 E4
na, country 45 H3		Easter Island 30 L6	French Guiana, province 29 F3	Great Salt Lake 22 D2	Helena 22 D1
sasibi 19 L3	Da Nang 45 J5	Eastern Ghats, mountains 44 F5	French Polynesia, country 30 J6	Great Salt Lake Desert 22 D3	Helsingborg 36 Q4
sinau 39 J2	Dacca 45 H4	Ebro, river 37 H11	Frio, Cape 28 G6	Great Sandy Desert 31 C3	Helsinki 35 M3
ta 41 D12	Daio, Cape 46 C4	Echo Bay 18 G2	Frisian Islands 36 L6	Great Slave Lake 18 G2	Herat 44 E3
ttagong 45 H4	Dakar 33 B4	Ecuador, country 29 D4	Fujiyama, mountain 46 C3	Great Victoria Desert 31 C4	Hermosillo 26 B2
istchurch 31 H12	Dalian 45 L3	Edinburgh 36 G5	Fukui 46 C3	Great Wall of China 45 J3	Himalayas, mountains 44 F3
ungking 45 J4	Dallas 23 G4	Edmonton 18 G3	Fukuoka 46 A4	Greater Antilles, islands 16 M7	Himeji 46 B4
urchill 18 J3	Damascus 44 B3	Egypt, country 33 F3	Fukushima 46 D3	Greece, country 39 H4	Hindu Kush, mountains 44 E3
irchill, river 18 J3	Danube, river 39 J3	El Aaiun 33 B3	Fundy, Bay of 19 M4	Greenland 16 Q2	Hino, Cape 46 B4
cinnati 23 K3	Dar es Salaam 33 G6	El Paso 22 E4	Fushun 45 L2	Grenada, country 27 M5	Hiroshima 46 B4
altepetl, mountain E4	Dardanelles 39 J4	El Salvador, country 26 F5	Fuzhou 45 K4	Grenoble 37 L10	Hispaniola, island 16 N8
dad Bolívar 27 M6	Darién, Gulf of 27 J6	Elba, island 37 P11		Groningen 36 L6	Hitachi 46 D3
dad Juarez 26 C1	Darling Range 31 B4	Elbe, river 36 P6	Gabon, country 33 E6	Groznyy 40 E5	Ho Chi Minh City 45 J5
ar, Cape 36 D7	Darling, river 31 E5	Elbert, Mount 22 E3	Gaborone 33 F8	Guadalajara 26 C3	Hobart 31 E12
rmont-Ferrand K10	Darwin 31 D9	Elbrus, mountain 40 E5	Galapagos Islands 29 C3	Guadalquivir, river 38 B4	Hoggar, mountains 32 D3
veland 23 K2	Dauphin 18 H3	Ellesmere Island 16 M2	Galati 39 J2	Guadeloupe, country 27 M4	Hokkaido, island 46 D2
-Napoca 39 H2	Davao 45 L6	Enderby Land 47 Q	Galway 36 D6	Guardafui, Cape 32 J4	Honduras, country 26 G5
st Mountains 18 E3	Davis Strait 19 M2	England, kingdom 36 G7	Gambia, country 33 B4	Guatemala, country 26 F4	Honduras, Gulf of 26 G4
st Ranges 22 B3	Dawson 18 E2	English Channel 36 G7	Gander 19 N4	Guatemala City 26 F5	Hong Kong 45 K4
ts Land 47 N	Dayton 23 K3	Equatorial Guinea, country 33 D5	Ganges, river 44 G4	Guaviare, river 27 K7	Honiara 31 F8
, Cape 23 N2	Death Valley 22 C3	Erfurt 36 N7	Garonne, river 37 H10	Guayaquil 29 D4	Honolulu 22 R8
mbatore 44 F3	Debrecen 39 H2	Erie, Lake 23 K2	Gävle 36 S2	Guernsey, island 37 F8	Honshu, island 46 C4
ogne 36 M7	Deccan, region 44 F5	Erimo, Cape 46 D2	Gaziantep 39 L4	Guiana Highlands 28 E3	Hormuz, Strait of 44 D4
ombia, country 29 D3	Delaware, state 25 L3	Eritrea, country 33 G4	Gdansk 35 L5	Guinea, country 33 B4	Houston 23 G5
ombo 44 F6	Delaware Bay 23 M3	Esbjerg 36 M5	Geneva 37 M9	Guinea, region 32 C5	Huambo 33 E7
orado Plateau 22 D3	Delhi 44 F4	Esfahan 44 D3	Geneva, Lake 37 L9	Guinea, Gulf of 33 B6	Hudson, river 23 M2
orado Springs 22 F3	Delphi 39 H4	Essen 36 M7	Genoa 37 M10	Guinea-Bissau, country 33 B4	Hudson Bay 19 K2
orado, river 22 D4	Denmark, country 36 N5	Essequibo, river 27 N7	Genoa, Gulf of 37 N11	Guiyang 45 J4	Hudson Strait 19 L2
orado, state 24 E3	Denver 22 F3	Estonia, country 35 M4	George Town 45 H6	Gulf, The 44 D4	Hungary, country 39 G2
umbia 23 K4	Des Moines 23 H2	Ethiopia, country 33 G5	Georgetown 27 M6	Guyana, country 27 M6	Huron, Lake 23 K2
umbia, river 22 B1	Detroit 23 K2	Ethiopian Highlands 32 G4	Georgia, country 40 E5	Gyandzha 40 E5	Hwang-Ho, river 45 K3
umbus (Georgia) K4	Dhaulagiri, mt. 44 G4	Etna, Mount 38 F4	Georgia, state 25 K4		Hyderabad (India) 44 F5
umbus (Ohio) 23 K3	Dijon 37 L9	Euphrates, river 44 C3	Georgian Bay 23 K1	Hachijo Island 46 C4	Hyderabad (Pakistan) 44 E4
nmunism Peak 40 F8	Dimitri Laptev Strait 41 B14	Europe, continent 35	Germany, country 36 M7	Hachinohe 46 D2	
norin, Cape 44 F6	Dinaric Alps, mountains 39 G3	Everest, Mount 44 G4	Ghana, country 33 C5	Hague, Cap de la 37 G8	Iasi 39 J2
noros, country 33 H7	Djibouti 33 H4	Everglades, region 23 K5	Ghats, Eastern, mountains 44 F5	Hague, The 36 K6	Iberian Peninsula 34 G6
akry 33 B4	Djibouti, country 33 H4	Eyre, Lake 31 D4	Ghats, Western, mountains 44 F4	Hailar 41 E12	Ibiza, island 37 J13
ncepcion 29 D7	Dnepr, river 39 K1		Ghent 36 K7	Hainan, island 45 K5	Iceland, country 34 C3
cord 23 M2	Dnepropetrovsk 39 K2	Fairbanks 22 W10	Gibraltar, country 37 E14	Haiphong 45 J4	Ichinomiya 46 C3
ngo, country 33 E6	Dnestr, river 39 J2	Faisalabad 44 E3	Gibraltar, Strait of 37 E14	Haiti, country 27 K4	Idaho, state 24 C2
ngo, river 32 F5	Dodecanese, islands 39 J4	Falkland Islands 29 E9	Gibson Desert 31 C4	Hakodate 46 D2	Igarka 40 C9
ngo, Democratic Rep. the, country 33 F5	Dodoma 33 G6	Farewell, Cape 19 P3	Gifu 46 C3	Halifax 19 M4	Ili, river 40 E8
ngo Basin 32 E5	Dominica, country 27 M4	Fargo 23 G1	Gijon 37 E11	Halle 36 Q7	Illinois, state 25 H3
nnecticut, state 25 M2	Dominican Republic, country 27 K4	Faroe Islands 36 E2	Gila, river 22 D4	Halmahera, island 45 L6	India, country 44 F4
stance, Lake 37 N9	Don, river 40 E5	Fear, Cape 23 L4	Gilbert Islands 30 G4	Hamamatsu 46 C4	Indian Ocean 13 N4
nstanta 39 J3	Donetsk 39 L2	Fehmarn, island 36 P5	Gironde, river 37 H10		Indian River 23 K5
ok Islands 30 H5	Dortmund 36 M7	Fiji, country 31 H9	Gizhiga 41 C17		Indiana, state 25 J2
ok, Aoraki Mount 31 G6	Douro, river 37 D12	Finland, country 35 M3	Glasgow 36 F5		Indianapolis 23 J3
penhagen 36 Q5	Dover (UK) 36 J7	Finland, Gulf of 35 M4	Gobi Desert 45 J2		Indigirka, river 41 C15
al Sea 31 F3	Dover (USA) 23 L3	Flensburg 36 M5	Godavari, river 44 F5		Indo-China, region 42 N7
doba (Argentina) E7	Drake Passage 47 Y	Flin Flon 18 H3	Goiana 29 F5		Indonesia, country 45 J7
doba (Spain) 37 F14	Drakensberg, mountains 32 F9	Flinders Ranges 31 D4	Gomel 39 K1		Indore 44 F4
fu, island 39 G4		Flinders, river 31 E3	Good Hope, Cape of 33 E9		Indus, river 44 E4
fu, Gulf of 39 H4		Florence 37 P11	Gothenburg 36 N4		
k 36 D7		Flores Sea 45 K7			
ner Brook 19 N4					
rientes, Cape 26 C3					

94

aimo 18 F4
chang 45 K4
cy 37 M8
king 45 K3
ning 45 J4
tes 37 H9
les 38 F3
odnaya, mountain
  C7
vik 35 L2
hville 23 J3
ssau 27 J2
amena 33 E4
raska, state 24 F2
ro, river 28 E3
sse, river 36 R7
son, river 18 J3
al, country 44 G4
s, Loch 36 F4
herlands, country
  K6
herlands Antilles,
  untry 27 L5
ada, state 24 C3
v Britain, island
  F2
v Brunswick,
  ovince 21 M4
v Caledonia
  ovince 31 G10
v Guinea, island
  D2
v Hampshire, state
  M2
v Ireland, island
  F2
v Jersey, state 25 M2
v Mexico, state 24 E4
v Orleans 23 J5
v Siberian Islands
  B14
v South Wales, state
  E11
v York 23 M2
v York, state 25 L2
v Zealand, country
  G11
vcastle (Australia)
  F11
vcastle (U.K.) 36 H5
vfoundland, island
  N4
vfoundland, province
  M3
mey 33 D4
aragua, country
  G5
e 37 M11
bar Islands 45 H6
osia 39 K4
er, country 33 D4
er, river 32 D4
eria, country 33 D5
slands 46 C4
ata 46 C3
au 22 P8
, Blue, river 32 G4
, river 32 G3
, White, river 32 G4
e, province 31 K9
ane Kolymsk 41 C17
neudinsk 41 D10
aniy Novgorod 40 D5
aniy Tagil 40 D7
eoka 46 B4
dvik 41 B12
folk 23 L3
folk Island 31 G4
lsk 41 C9
rköping 36 R3
th America,
  ntinent 16

North Bay 19 L4
North Cape
  (New Zealand) 31 H5
North Cape (Norway)
  35 M1
North Carolina, state
  25 K3
North Dakota, state
  24 F1
North Dvina, river 40 C5
North European Plain
  34 L4
North Island 31 G5
North Korea, country
  45 L2
North Magnetic Pole
  47 L
North Platte, river 22 F2
North Pole 47 D
North Sea 36 J4
North West Cape 31 B4
Northern Ireland,
  province 36 E5
Northern Marianas,
  country 30 F4
Northwest Territories
  20 F2
Norway, country 35 J3
Norwegian Sea 47 H
Norwich 36 J6
Noshiro 46 C2
Nottingham 36 H6
Nouakchott 33 B4
Noumea, Island 31 G10
Nova Scotia, province
  21 M4
Novaya Zemlya, island
  40 B6
Novokuznetsk 40 D9
Novosibirsk 40 D8
Novy Port 40 C8
Nullarbor Plain 31 C5
Numazu 46 C3
Nunavut, territory 20 H2
Nuremburg 37 P8
Nuuk 19 N2

Oahu 22 R8
Ob, river 40 C7
Ob, Gulf of 40 C8
Obihiro 46 D2
October Revolution
  Island 41 B11
Odense 36 N5
Oder, river 36 R6
Odessa 39 K2
Ohio, river 23 J3
Ohio, state 25 K2
Oita 46 B4
Oka, river 40 D5
Okayama 46 B4
Okeechobee, Lake 23 K5
Okhotsk 41 D15
Okhotsk, Sea of 41 D15
Oki Islands 46 B3
Oklahoma, state 24 G3
Oklahoma City 22 G3
Okushiri 46 C2
Olekminsk 41 C13
Olenek, river 41 B13
Olympia 39 H4
Olympia, Mount 22 B1
Olympus, Mount 39 H3
Omaha 23 G2
Oman, country 44 D5
Oman, Gulf of 44 D4
Omiya 46 C3
Omsk 40 D8
Omuta 46 B4

Onega, Lake 40 C4
Ontario, Lake 23 L2
Ontario, province 21 J3
Oporto 37 D12
Oral 40 D6
Orange, river 33 E8
Orebro 36 R3
Oregon, state 24 B2
Orel 40 D4
Orenburg 40 D6
Orinoco, river 27 M6
Orkney Islands 36 G3
Orlando 23 K5
Orléans 38 J9
Orsk 40 D6
Osaka 46 C4
Oslo 36 N3
Osnabrück 36 M6
Osumi Channel 46 B4
Otaru 46 D2
Ottawa 19 L4
Ottawa, river 23 L1
Ouagadougou 33 C4
Owen Stanley Range
  31 E2
Oxford 36 H7
Ozark Plateau 23 H3
Ozarks, Lake of the
  23 H3

Pacaraima, Sierra 27 M7
Pacific Ocean 30 G3
Padang 45 H7
Pakistan, country 44 E4
Palau, country 30 E4
Palawan 45 K6
Palembang 45 J7
Palermo 38 F4
Palma 37 K13
Palmas, Cape 32 C5
Pamir, mountains 44 F3
Pamlico Sound 23 L3
Pampas, region 28 E7
Panama 27 H6
Panama, country 27 H6
Panama Canal 29 D2
Panama, Gulf of 27 J6
Panama, Isthmus of
  16 M8
Papua New Guinea,
  country 31 E8
Paraguay, country 29 E6
Paraguay, river 28 F6
Paramaribo 29 F3
Parana, river 28 F6
Parinas, Point 28 C4
Paris 37 K8
Parma 37 P10
Patagonia, region 28 D9
Patna 44 G4
Pátrai 39 H4
Pavlodar 40 D8
Peace, river 18 G3
Pechora, river 40 C6
Pecos, river 22 F4
Peking = Beijing 45 K3
Peloponnese, region
  39 H4
Pennsylvania, state
  25 L2
Penza 40 D5
Penzance 36 E7
Perm 35 U4
Perpignan 37 K11
Persian Gulf = The Gulf
  44 D4
Perth 31 B11
Peru, country 29 D5
Petropavlovsk
  Kamchatskiy 41 D16
Petrozavodsk 40 C3

Philadelphia 23 M2
Philippines, country
  45 L5
Phnom Penh 45 J5
Phoenix 22 D4
Phoenix Islands 30 H5
Pierre 22 F2
Pindus Mountains 39 H3
Pisa 37 P11
Pitcairn Island 30 K6
Pittsburgh 23 K2
Ploiesti 39 J3
Plovdiv 39 H3
Plymouth 36 F7
Plzen 36 Q8
Po, river 37 P10
Pohang 46 A3
Pointe-à-Pitre 27 M4
Poitiers 37 H9
Poland, country 35 L5
Polar Plateau 47 Y
Polynesia, region 30 H4
Pompei 38 F3
Pontchartrain, Lake
  23 H4
Pontianak 45 J6
Pontine Mountains
  39 K3
Popocatepetl, mountain
  26 D4
Port-au-Prince 27 J4
Port Elizabeth 33 F9
Port Moresby 31 E8
Port of Spain 27 M5
Port Sudan 33 G3
Port Vila 31 G9
Portage la Prairie 18 H3
Portland (Maine) 23 M2
Portland (Oregon) 22 B1
Porto Alegre 29 G6
Porto Novo 33 C5
Portsmouth 36 H7
Portugal, country 37 D13
Potomac, river 23 L3
Potsdam 36 Q6
Poznan 39 G1
Prague 36 Q7
Pretoria 33 F8
Prince Albert 18 H3
Prince Edward Island,
  province 21 M4
Prince George 18 F3
Prince of Wales Island
  18 H1
Prince Rupert 18 F3
Pripet, river 39 J1
Providence 23 M2
Prut, river 39 J2
Prydz Bay 47 R
Puebla 27 J4
Puerto Rico, country
  27 L4
Pune 44 F5
Punta Arenas 29 D9
Pusan 45 L3
Pyongyang 45 L3
Pyrenees, mountains
  37 H11

Qandahar 44 E3
Qatar, country 44 D4
Qingdao 45 K3
Qiqihar 45 L2
Québec 19 L4
Québec, province 21 L3
Queen Charlotte Islands
  18 E3
Queen Elizabeth Islands
  17 F1
Queen Maud Land 47 P

Queensland, state
  31 E10
Quetta 44 E3
Quezon City 45 L5
Quito 29 D4

Rabat 33 C2
Race, Cape 19 N4
Rainier, Mount 22 B1
Raleigh 23 L3
Rangoon 45 H5
Rankin Inlet 18 J2
Ravenna 37 Q10
Rebun, island 46 D1
Recife 29 H4
Red, river 23 H4
Red Deer 18 G3
Red Sea 44 B5
Regina 18 H3
Reindeer Lake 18 H3
Rennes 37 H8
Reno 22 C3
Réunion, island 32 J8
Revilla Gigedo Islands
  26 B4
Reykjavik 34 B3
Rhine, river 36 M7
Rhode Island, state
  25 M2
Rhodes, island 39 J4
Rhodope, mountains
  39 H3
Rhône, river 37 L10
Richmond 23 L3
Rift Valley, Great 32 G6
Riga 35 M4
Riishiri, island 46 D1
Rimini 38 F3
Rimouski 19 M4
Rio de Janeiro 29 G6
Rio de la Plata, estuary
  28 F7
Rio Grande de Santiago,
  river 26 C3
Rio Grande, river 22 F5
Riyadh 44 C4
Roanoke, river 23 L3
Robson, Mount 18 G3
Rochester 23 L2
Rockhampton 31 F10
Rocky Mountains 16 H4
Romania, country 39 H2
Rome 37 P12
Roraima, Mount 27 M6
Rosario 29 E7
Ross Sea 47 V
Rostock 36 Q6
Rostov 39 L2
Rotterdam 36 K7
Rouen 38 J8
Rub' al Khali, region
  44 C5
Rügen, island 36 Q5
Russia, country 40 C6
Rwanda, country 33 F6
Ryazan 40 D5
Rybinsk 40 D4
Ryukyu Islands 45 L4

Sabah 45 K6
Sabine, river 23 G4
Sable Island 19 N4
Sable, Cape (Canada)
  19 M4
Sable, Cape (USA) 23 K5
Sacramento 22 B3
Sacramento Mountains
  22 E4
Sacramento Valley
  22 B2

Sado, island 46 C3
Sahara, desert 32 B4
Sahel, region 32 C4
St.-Étienne 37 K10
St. George's Channel
  36 E7
St. Helena, island 33 C7
St. Helens, Mount 22 B1
St. John 19 M4
St. John's (Antigua)
  27 M4
St. John's (Canada)
  19 N4
St. Kitts-Nevis, country
  27 M4
St. Lawrence, Gulf of
  19 M4
St. Lawrence, river
  19 M4
St. Louis 23 H3
St. Lucia, country 27 M5
St.-Nazaire 37 G9
St. Paul 23 H2
St. Petersburg 35 P4
St. Pierre & Miquelon,
  islands 21 N4
St. Vincent & the
  Grenadines, country
  27 M5
St. Vincent, Cape 37 D14
Sakai 46 C4
Sakata 46 C3
Sakhalin, island 41 D15
Salem 22 B2
Salt Lake City 22 D2
Salton Sea 22 C4
Salvador 29 H5
Salween, river 45 H5
Salzburg 37 Q9
Samara 35 T5
Samarkand 40 F7
Samoa Islands 31 J3
Samos, island 39 J4
Samsun 39 L3
San Andreas Fault 22 B3
San Antonio 22 G5
San Bernardino 22 C4
San Blas, Cape 23 J5
San Diego 22 C4
San Francisco 22 B3
San Joaquin Valley
  22 B3
San José 27 H6
San Juan 27 L4
San Lucas, Cape 26 B3
San Marino 37 Q11
San Pedro Sula 26 G4
San Salvador 26 F5
San Sebastian 37 G11
Sana 44 C5
Santa Cruz Islands
  31 G2
Santa Fe 22 E3
Santander 37 F11
Santiago (Chile) 29 D7
Santiago (Dominican
  Republic) 27 K4
Santiago de Cuba 27 J4
Santo Domingo 27 K4
São Francisco, river
  28 G4
São Paulo 29 F6
Sao Roque, Cape 28 H4
Sao Tome & Principe,
  country 33 D5
Saône, river 37 L9
Sapporo 46 D2
Sarajevo 39 G3
Saratov 40 D5
Sarawak, province 45 K6
Sardinia, island 37 N12
Sasebo 46 A4